Lionel

The Ted Wragg Guide to Education

Thank God for Ted Wragg. His humour is a tonic and an inspiration: the sort that has you gnashing your teeth with rage one minute and clutching your sides with laughter the next. This book should be part of the National Curriculum for anyone who wants to know about education, and required reading for rational beings and ministers alike.

Rory Bremner

As fast as the unintended blunders of bureaucrats and ministers sap the energy, idealism and commitment of the teaching profession, so Ted Wragg's Friday back page column refuels their determination to stick to their life's work . . .. With his column, and his example at Exeter in research and in the training and education of teachers, Ted Wragg has achieved more for real improvement in the classroom than all the effort of twenty pieces of legislation, eight Secretaries of State and thousands of circulars . . .. Ted's secret seems to be able to place himself, apparently without effort, in anyone's shoes, especially those of teachers. He has the uncanny knack of creating energy, humour and generosity as fast as others unwittingly consume it.

Professor Tim Brighouse, Chief Education Officer,
Birmingham City Council

Ted Wragg writes about education (and a lot of other things) with a combination of wit, passion and knowledge that is not equalled by anyone else. The 'Guide' should be compulsory reading for Secretaries of State – even those with learning difficulties would benefit.

Neil Kinnock

Ted Wragg's column has been essential reading for those who think education too important to be left in the hands of the politicians. At a time when third rate people have arrogated to themselves unprecedented powers over how children think and how teachers behave, Wragg has been one of the few voices that has courageously and consistently pricked the politicians' pomposity and exposed their cynical disregard for educational values.

Professor Richard Pring, Director,
University of Oxford Department of Educational Studies

The Ted Wragg Guide to Education

Ted Wragg

Illustrated by Nigel Paige

BUTTERWORTH
HEINEMANN

Butterworth-Heinemann Ltd
Linacre House, Jordan Hill, Oxford OX2 8DP

$\mathcal{R}$ A member of the Reed Elsevier plc group

OXFORD   LONDON   BOSTON
MUNICH   NEW DELHI   SINGAPORE   SYDNEY
TOKYO   TORONTO   WELLINGTON

First published 1995

British Library Cataloguing in Publication Data
A catalogue record for this book is available from
the British Library

ISBN 0 7506 2431 0

Composition by Genesis Typesetting, Laser Quay, Rochester, Kent
Printed and bound in Great Britain by Biddles Ltd, Guildford and
Kings Lynn

Contents

Introduction

'Did it really happen?' When twenty-first century historians come to write the definitive account of life in twentieth century Britain, their readers will gasp in disbelief at some of the events in education during the last two decades of the twentieth century. Well it did happen. Like thousands of other bewildered members of the education profession, I was there. So I have always wanted to bring together some of the articles I wrote between the early-1980s and the mid-1990s in the *Times Educational Supplement* that chronicled these incredible years. There have been separate books of my articles over a two-year period, but never a collection covering the whole desperate fifteen or so years.

It was a time when ministers clambered over each other to out-loony their predecessors. 'Me Tarzan, you scum' was the message to teachers. Right-wing think tanks, quangos, performance indicators, and propaganda replaced intelligent debate, democratic processes and artistry. As with the Hydra, when you shredded one silly bureaucratic document, another even dafter one arrived in the following day's post. As fast as I wrote what I thought was some lyrical piece of crazed fantasy in the *Times Educational Supplement*, a real life event would trump it. Satirists didn't stand a chance against the competition.

People often ask me for copies of articles which are now out of print, like 'KJ the movie', which described how Sir Keith Joseph reminded me of ET, the extra-terrestrial creature in Steven Spielberg's Hollywood blockbuster, or 'Who put the ass in assessment?', which satirized the documents on national testing. I have tried to include a wide selection of articles, starting back in Sir Keith Joseph's time in the early 1980s and coming right up to many articles which have not been published in book form before, recording the mid-1990s, when the National Curriculum was revised and sanity was supposed to be restored. The first four chapters describe political events in chronological order, the last five chapters address key themes like curriculum, teachers, management and organization.

Ted Wragg

1

Sir Monty Python

The years up to 1986 were dominated by Margaret Thatcher and Sir Keith Joseph, or Sir Monty Python as I used to call his *alter ego*. It was the beginning of what turned out for many teachers to be a long nightmare – Mrs Thatcher reminded one of Barbara Woodhouse training dogs; Norman Tebbit threatened to set up his own vocational schools; privatization, league tables and state control began to make an appearance; and the right-wing think tanks started to think, or whatever it was they did.

KJ the movie

Like everyone else I was totally entranced by Steven Spielberg's blockbusting box-office super-success fantasy film about the wizened extra-terrestrial creature left behind by his spacecraft who became Secretary of State for Education.

Despite the intense Hollywood hype, the film *KJ* really is, as several film critics have pointed out, a modern classic fairy-tail or pantomine, and it is small wonder that a multi-million dollar industry has grown out of it selling KJ dolls, KJ key rings, KJ T-shirts and KJ exercise book covers. One enterprising firm has even started selling teachers KJ sticks of chalk, the ends of which are shaped in the familiar wrinkled KJ puzzled features. It disintegrates when used.

I do not want to spoil the fun for those few who have not yet managed to see the actual film, but *KJ* so moves the audience to laughter and tears that I am sure filmgoers will be trying to explain its success for years to come. Incidentally it is much more enjoyable to see the film in a cinema rather than watch one of the poor quality illicit videos currently circulating. Months ago I was offered just such a pirate copy by a DES civil servant in a dirty Christian Dior mac with the X-rated *Confessions of a Mandarin* on the flip side, but I turned it down.

The film *KJ* has all the ingredients of the classic fairy tale: a central character bewildered at the beginning of the film to find himself in alien surroundings at the DES, two oriental villains Boi-Son and Norm-An who pretend to befriend him, and a gormless clown Willee, brilliantly played by an unknown but rising star, junior education minister William Shelton, fresh from his triumph in the latest British comedy *Carry on Cretin*. There is even a blonde heroine, Marg, newly returned from a crying tour of Europe where she wept at the Berlin Wall, blubbered at the EEC summit meeting, and cascaded in tears at the DES after the Clegg salary award.

Even before KJ has learned to speak any words at all people in the audience are on the edge of the seats, wondering whether successive deputations from the NUT, NAS, NAHT, local authorities and university vice chancellors will spot that he is an outer-galactic alien, but fortunately for us they take his total silence to all their pleas to be either obstinacy or profound reflection, and to our relief he survives a few early scares.

One of the most moving moments in the film comes when he utters his initial croaking attempts at speech. Under tuition from the faithful Marg he slowly articulates his words 'KJ phone home'. Unfortunately British Telecom and the DES switchboard connect him to the Speaking Clock, so he makes it a junior minister.

Undeterred he uses his immense brain power to construct a transgalactic communication device from a few bits of metal and some string, which successfully links him with his fellow extra-terrestrials. At this moment in the film I am not ashamed to say that we adults in the cinema, fingers tightly around the throat of our KJ dolls, were close to tears. Marg was up to her waist in them. Thinking, as ever, of the children, KJ promptly persuades the MSC to provide thousands of unemployed proles to mass-produce his metal and string communication device and spends four billion pounds of DES money installing one in every school, in case pupils should wish to phone the planet Zarg.

Meanwhile the evil oriental duo, Boi-Son and Norm-An, while feigning friendship, seek to discredit KJ. Boi-Son, to hisses and boos from the audience, persuades KJ that in order to return home he needs to invest vast sums of money buying a set of vouchers (Oh yes he does, oh no he doesn't). Norm-An tells him that, if only he will believe, he can sit astride a bicycle and fly through the air like Mary Poppins. Unfortunately he roman candles straight into the Thames, as Norm-An has given him a rucksack instead of a parachute.

The climax of the film comes as a team of doctors debate if it is scientifically possible for someone with a zero EEG reading to function as a minister, when in bounds Willee, the gormless clown, confirming that it is. At this moment KJ revives, sits bolt upright, puts Willee in charge of information technology, though neither knows what it is, and announces over and over again in his croaky voice, 'KJ go home, KJ go home'.

Finally, to the immense relief of the audience, and I saw hard-bitten teacher unionists and chief education officers on their feet unashamedly cheering at this point, KJ is finally rescued. The kindly and attentive Marg, loyal to the last, helps him aboard the spacecraft, and, a shoe on each ear and jacket on back to front, he leaves the DES to the sound of the *KJ* theme. At last Baron KJ is reunited with his fellows in the House of Lords four million light years away, and the pantomime season is over.

14 January 1983

The Thatchhouse way

Good evening viewers, and welcome to another programme in my series, *Training Ministers the Thatchhouse Way*. This week, we've brought the travelling roadshow to a large field at the back of the Department of Education and Science, and as usual, we'll start with a bit of basic obedience work, and then look at a few problem cases. So quiet everybody, please, and I'll ask one or two civil servants to bring out their Education Ministers so we can put them through their paces.

Now, what's this one called? Keith. Jolly good. Here Keith. *Good boy.* Just run him round on a loose lead. No dear, not too tight, just drape your lead loosely over two fingers of your right hand and if he gets out of line, give him a quick jerk on the choker and say 'Heel' in a rough voice. Jolly good. That's fine.

Did you say Keith was a problem, dear. Yes? What does he do? He's completely crackers. Yes, I see. Could you be a bit more specific, dear? He comes up with crazy ideas every day and you would like him to be locked up somewhere. Well, we can't do that I'm afraid. Come here Keith. Roll over. Good boy. Give me a silly idea then Keith . . . the voucher scheme . . . would cost £150m a year bureaucracy alone, and give no one any more choice than they have now. *There's a clever boy.* Did you see how I tickled his tummy viewers? There you are dear, take him back to the others and keep humouring him. Who's next?

Goodness me, this is a shy little one. What's his name? William who? William Shelton. Come here Will, here boy. Just run him round, so the viewers can see him. Loosen the choker please, just use two finger of your right hand, that's quite enough. No, don't jerk his choker too hard – he looks frightened to death, poor thing. Jolly good. Bring him over here, and turn him to face the camera. Let me just give him my scent. Oh dear, that's terrified him.

Now, what's William's problem? Nobody has heard of him, and he knows absolutely nothing about education . . . I see . . . here William. Sit. Let's hear you say in a big voice, 'I'm William Shelton. I'm an education minister'. Dear me, he's forgotten it already. Well viewers, remember, if your first command is too difficult give a little teeny tug with just two fingers on the choke chain and repeat it in a simpler form. Now, *big* voice, William; say 'I'm William Shelton'. No, don't roll over William. Sit. Good boy. Now, big voice, 'I'm William'. Quiet everybody, you'll confuse him. Here boy, *Big* voice, say, 'I'm'. No I'm awfully sorry viewers, he's forgotten. Never mind, keep working him on a loose choker, and we'll return him to oblivion as soon as we can.

Who's next? Hello, what's this little scoundrel called then? Another William. Here boy, William Waldegrave. That's a big name for a little chappie. Now, what's little Willy's problem? He's very clever, I see, and he doesn't like closing colleges of education. Here Willy. Sit. *Clever* boy. Will someone bring out a college principal please. Jolly good, now you stand here in front of the camera Willy, and say in a big rough voice, 'Close'. No, no. That's much too weedy. Again, big, deep voice Willy. *'Close'*. That's better. Just run him round with two fingers loosely on his choke chain, and keep telling him how clever he is.

Goodness, who have we got here? This is a big rough, shaggy thing, isn't he ladies and gentlemen? Run him round on a loose lead so the viewers can see him. Gosh he's all over the place. What's his name? Rhodes, here boy. No, come away from that tree, Rhodes. *Naughty* boy. Give him a really firm tug on his choker if he does that sort of thing in public.

Now dear, what kind of problems are you having with Rhodes? I see, he's too rough and everyone laughs at him. Of course that will make him behave in a very silly way. Now watch carefully viewers, I'm going to blow up his nose. Good boy, Rhodes. Where is his nose?

He has another problem, has he dear? His inspectors are too independent. They don't like inspecting, but when they do they always criticize the Government for not providing enough money. Let's see if we can cure that. Right, can someone bring forward an HMI. Put him *down* Rhodes, *naughty* boy. If he bites anyone again, dear, just give him a sharp dig with your elbow. Now Rhodes, let me hear you say, 'Inspect', No, no, you must stress the 't' sound at the end. Again, 'Inspect . . .t'. That's better. Now, follow that up with, 'Suppress'. No no, Rhodes, bring out the hiss at the end 'Suppressss'. That's jolly good.

What, he's got yet *another* problem? He doesn't know how to handle teachers properly. Goodness me, I've told you enough times in this programme how to deal with teachers. Just two fingers, Rhodes.

5 November 1982

Sir Monty's choice

'Good morning minister, we've come to bring you the application forms for the vacant post of Senior Chief Inspector of Schools. Quite a lot of people have applied for it, and we need to decide fairly soon who should be appointed to this very important post.'

'Indeed, indeed. Do come in gentlemen, sit down and make yourselves comfortable. Would one of you mind switching off the recording of Götterdämmerung, and make sure you don't trip over my roller skates, only there's a teachers' union delegation coming to see me in a few minutes and I want to look my best.'

'Thank you, minister. There have been some really excellent applications, and it is vital that we appoint someone of outstanding ability to head the Inspectorate.'

'Splendid, splendid. But tell me, why have you brought all the applications to me?'

'Because the Secretary of State has to make the final decision on these matters.'

'Well then, why not take the application forms to him?'

'But you are the Secretary of State, minister.'

'Am I? I thought I was Sir Keith Joseph.'

'You are indeed minister, but you are also the Secretary of State for Education.'

'Bless my soul. Well, in that case let us waste no more time. Tell me about the applications you have received.'

'They are of the highest quality, and in addition we have been given a list of strongly recommended people who have not formally applied.'

'Well known people with distinction in their field?'

'Yes minister. Several names were sent in, and there was quite a lot of support for Brian Clough.'

'Is he an HMI?'

'No, he's the manager of Nottingham Forest.'

'We must keep an open mind on these matters. I am sure someone with Forestry Commission experience could be very useful. Any other recommendations?'

'Well minister, you did say at a previous meeting that you would give thought to one or two of your own friends.'

'Ah yes. I think most of my friends have got jobs already. Let me see, David Young is in charge of the MSC, and then his brother Stuart Young has become Chairman of the BBC. I've got a feeling that there's another brother called Alfred, or perhaps Arthur Young.'

'I wouldn't know minister.'

'Failing that they've an awfully nice next door neighbour called Colonel Postlethwaite, or is it Captain Perryweather, blessed if I can remember. Then there's Mary Whitehouse.'

'You were thinking of making her Chairman of the new Curriculum Council, minister, when Cliff Richard turned it down.'

'Indeed. By the way, what sort of salary are we offering for this appointment?'

'The post was advertised at £30,250 which consists of a basic salary of £30,000 and an additional £250 Librium allowance.'

'Good. I hope that is more than someone would get on the dole, I mean we must offer an incentive to people to go to work.'

'The money is distinctly above what people obtain on the dole, minister.'

'Excellent. I am sure we shall have no difficulty making a good appointment. Now what about my political assistant, young Oliver Letwin, he's a splendid fellow?'

'I think, minister, there would be resentment from the HMI if someone so young and fresh out of school and university himself were appointed. There might also be a problem of credibility with the teaching profession in view of certain incidents during his visits to schools.'

'Incidents, what do you mean?'

'You remember, minister, during his visit to East Swineshire comprehensive some pupils were eating their beefburgers and ketchup, and he asked them if there was enough basil in the fricadelles de veau à la Nicoise. Then he complained to the head that the second year remedial class had only a rudimentary knowledge of Wittgenstein's Tractatus.'

'Well couldn't we give him the job under the Youth Training Scheme and arrange for day release?'

'I think there may be pressure to pay all YTS trainees £30,000 a year if we did that, minister.'

'No matter, we have a splendid list of people, so let me sum up. Our first choice is your Forestry Commission chappie. Then there is Alfred or Arthur Young. If that falls through or if he does not exist then we offer it to Colonel Postlethwaite or Captain Perryweather. I told you it would be easy.'

'In all honesty minister, I must say that we have actually found it extremely difficult talking to you about this important matter.'

'Difficult talking to me about the appointment of the next Senior Chief Inspector of Schools. I fail to understand. Come on, out with it man. Why on earth should it be so difficult?'

'Well, minister, I don't quite know how to put this, but I think the fact that we are sitting down here in chairs while you are doing a headstand on top of your wardrobe might have something to do with it.'

22 April 1983

Crackpot Schemes Department

'Hello, is that the DES?' I want to enquire about the voucher scheme.'

'Certainly sir, luncheon, travel or Xmas Club?'

'No, I mean the educational voucher scheme, you know, the one Sir Keith Joseph is keen on which would give parents a thousand pound voucher they could cash in at the school of their choice.'

'Just a minute sir, I'll put you through to Mr Blandly-Smiling. He's in charge of the Minister's Crackpot Schemes Department. They might take a bit of time to answer, by the way, because it is right down in the basement where the Minister goes to do his thinking, and it's got padded walls.'

'Hello, Minister's Crackpot Schemes Department, Blandly-Smiling here. Can I help you?'

'Yes, I wonder if you can tell me how far the voucher scheme has got. I read in the press that Sir Keith Joseph wanted to push it through in time for the next election.'

'Well, unfortunately Sir Monty has not been around the DES for the last day or two. Rumour has it he's been standing as Screaming Lord Python of the Raving Loony Party in the Bermondsey by-election.'

'But do you think a voucher scheme would ever work?'

'Ours not to reason why, friend. We public servants are only here to implement the wishes and whims of our political masters. If Sir

Monty were to come in tomorrow and propose that a big dipper should be installed in every classroom in Britain, and that incidentally would represent one of his better ideas, it would be our job to devise a way of doing it. Our colleagues at the Ministry of Defence are currently working out a voucher scheme for the military, so you'll soon be able to club together with your neighbours and buy your own Sherman tank.'

'Didn't I read that the Cabinet wanted a more radical voucher scheme?'

'Ah, now Sir Monty was in Miss Piggy's bad books for once, because we had persuaded him the voucher scheme would only work for the private sector. Furthermore, several of the Cabinet were in a bad mood. For example, Heseltine had just been knocked down by the women of Greenham Common and was running around in tears claiming he'd been raped or something. Press reports merely said he had got up shaken but not stirred, and eye witnesses swore he actually tripped over his wig.'

'So is anyone working out all the details of it?'

'Indeed. You may have read in the papers that the voucher scheme is now in the hands of Sir Monty's recently hired 20-odd-year-old ex-Etonian political assistant Oliver Letwin. The trouble is young Olly has never been near a state school in his life. We've sent him out to one or two middle-of-the-road compers to let him see the snotty-nosed brigade at first hand, but the poor devil has been so sheltered from the proletariat he comes in looking shell-shocked after each visit.'

'Can't someone tell him how ordinary people live?'

'Well I've been assigned to further his education so I decided to take him on a bus to let him see what public transport was like, but he just sat there like a prune, stared in bewilderment at his bus ticket, and finally put it in his ear. When we escorted him on his first ever visit to Tesco, he hid behind a circle of trolleys with a wire basket over his head in case the natives attacked.'

'But isn't the scheme supposed to give parents a wider choice of school for their child?'

'I'll be honest with you, it's a huge con trick. In theory, you see, each punter can cash his voucher at any school he chooses. Now, can you imagine what the head of Eton is going to say when a few million smellies show up saying they prefer his outfit to Little Piddlington Secondary Modern?'

'I thought the major claim for vouchers was that popular schools could use them to build extra buildings, and that unpopular schools would thus starve to death.'

'Needless to say once a popular school has built prefabs all over its playgrounds and football pitch it immediately becomes unpopular. Parents then defect elsewhere leaving the school looking like Butlins in February, until a fleet of lorries cart off the prefabs up the M1 to the nearest fashionable school. The Watford Gap services lorry park is going to be packed out with unemployed teachers trying to hitch to a job in a portable school, and most of the lads round here are feverishly buying shares in the Portakabin industry.'

'But didn't Rhodes Boyson say parents could use vouchers to start their own school?'

'My advice would be to spend three hundred quid on a BBC microcomputer and pocket the change. Look squire, I'm sorry I must dash now, we've got to take young Olly to another comprehensive school and you wouldn't believe how excited he is.'

'Because it's such a good school?'

'No, because we've promised to take him there on the Tube.'

25 February 1983

Nineteen Eighty-four

In four weeks' time everyone will be speculating just how wide of the mark George Orwell was in his book *Nineteen Eighty-four*. In case you have forgotten here are some extracts from it . . .

It was a bright cold day in April, and the clocks were striking thirteen. Winston Smith hurried quickly through the glass doors of Victory Proletarian School where he was a teacher. Ahead of him on the corridor wall was a huge picture of a face. It was one of those pictures where the eyes follow you about when you move. BIG MONTY IS WATCHING YOU, the caption beneath it ran.

Once in the staffroom Winston stared out of the window at the enormous pyramidal structure of glittering white concrete across the road. It was the Ministry of Silly Curricula – Emmess C in Newspeak, the official language of Oceania. Winston reflected whether its lack of windows was to stop its bureaucrats committing hara-kiri. He reached across for his cup of Victory coffee. The taste was revolting, as it had been ever since the Ministry of Plenty had sacked all the dinner ladies as an economy measure.

By his left elbow lay his April stick of Victory chalk. Winston drummed it absent-mindedly on the staffroom table, whereupon it disintegrated to a fine powder. He sat gazing stupidly at it, wondering how to explain to the Ministry of Plenty official that he would need his May stick of chalk a month early. Meanwhile the telescreen on the wall droned out endless figures explaining how much more money was being spent on education than ever before.

On his way to his first lesson, he passed O'Brien the deputy head. 'It's nearly eleven hundred, time for Two Minutes Hate', O'Brien reminded him. Suddenly a picture of the Plowden Report appeared on every giant telescreen, followed by a picture of a 1960s progressive primary school classroom. Urged on by O'Brien, teachers began to chant 'Hate, hate, hate', one even hurling a copy of *Prevocational Maths* at the screen.

Once inside the classroom, Winston relaxed. He took from a pocket the last precious fragment of his March stick of chalk and wondered whether to assert his freedom by writing *DOWN WITH MONTY* on his blackboard. Instead he wrote $2 + 2 = 5$ and stood back to admire his own courage.

Seconds later he froze with terror. The door opened and in walked a member of the Emmess C Thought Police. He had never been so surprised since the day he had responded to a whole-page advert urging people to join the Peace Movement and found himself in the Army.

He remembered that a pupil, a fanatical member of the Junior Anti-sex League, had denounced him for one of his prevocational French lessons. 'Now, 6079 Smith W', began the Thought Policeman, 'what's all this about?'

Winston muttered an indistinct reply and then noticed to his horror that the Thought Policeman was staring at the $2 + 2 = 5$ he had written on the blackboard. This could mean redeployment as a PE Advisor. 'Ah, well done Smith', beamed the Thought Policeman. 'Keep hammering the basics and I'll consider sending a favourable report on you to the Ministry of Love.'

The new name for the DES still sounded strange to him, but Winston could not believe his lucky escape as he handed out pieces of used wallpaper for his prevocational poetry class to write on. He looked around the blank proletarian faces of his pupils. Most of the better-off parents had opted out of Victory Proletarian School and topped up their educational vouchers to buy places at private academies. All that was left was what were called dumb masses, pursuing a series of disparate anodyne prevocational courses for vocations that did not exist. The Victory prevocational poetry book decreed that today's assignment was to write a poem about either gaspipes or an overhead camshaft.

At that moment O'Brien walked in. The class fell silent. 'Report to Room 101, Smith', he bellowed. Winston's heart sank. 'But what have I done . . .?' 'Don't argue man. You know Big Monty does not approve of you discussing the social aspects of science in your prevocational physics class. Report to Room 101.'

In a daze Winston staggered down the corridor escorted by two men in white coats. He had heard all about Room 101 where the pain was not only unspeakable but personal; the torture was whatever each individual dreaded most.

'You have a choice', said O'Brien turning the knob of a giant telescreen. 'Either you read the Ministry of Love pamphlet *A Framework for the Curriculum*, or every single booklet produced by the Further Education Unit on Basically Basic Basics, or – this', and as he leapt aside the telescreen burst into life with a repeat of Big Monty being interviewed on *Panorama*. 'No, no, not the trading base speech again', blubbered Winston, 'I give in, I give in'. He had won the victory over himself. He loved Big Monty.

2 December 1983

Sir Keith: epilogue

There is a phase in life known as pre-retirement. It is those twilight years of a working career when some people prematurely hang up their boots and spend their time crossing days off the calendar or throwing darts at photographs of the boss.

There are other kinds of pre-retirement phenomena. One common state is that demob happiness when nothing can be taken seriously. A delirious head once told me: 'I'll sign anything at the moment, because six weeks from now I'm fireproof'. Her corridor was jammed with smiling teachers clutching scraps of paper and order forms.

Sir Keith Joseph manifested a third type of pre-retirement behaviour, that of the epitaph writer, for it is not unknown for distinguished people in positions of leadership to spend the last few years of their career imagining their eventual obituary. It was especially vital for Sir Keith to quit on a winning brief when he arrived at the DES in September 1981, because the press had labelled him as the dotty minister who, in his previous incarnations, had not only endorsed high-rise flats, but also rescued lame ducks in industry after preaching the need for government abstinence. He arrived eager to *do* something.

Back in 1981 the bookmakers, had they taken bets on these unpredictable matters, might well have offered evens on Sir Keith's chances of winning the Epitaph Stakes. After all, he succeeded a string of ministers whose impact on education had been about as potent as a speck of dust landing on the Pacific.

Fred Mulley infuriated his officials by protesting that the only power he had was to close temporary buildings in school playgrounds; Shirley Williams was loveable, talked a good game, but failed to deliver; and Mark Carlisle never got beyond tens and units. Only a pulled hamstring, it seemed, could prevent Sir Keith cantering up the home straight and collecting his winner's sash and pension book, before being driven off to a well-earned timeless graze in the House of Lords.

Evaluating Sir Keith's achievements these past four-and-half years is like filling in a profile on a student who gets marks of A or E with little in between. After Fred Carlisle and Mark Prentice, or was it Reg Mulley?, the memory plays cruel tricks with these non-entities – a reforming minister was quite a change, and reform he did, with the vigour of a thinking zealot. Even if one did not endorse his every move, he must deserve grade As for his courage in grasping the nettle of 16-plus examination reform, expressing more than concern for the bottom 40 per cent, rescuing technical education when it was in danger of slipping off the curriculum, trying to improve the quality of teaching and teacher education, strengthening parents' rights, ending the politicians' stranglehold on governing bodies, and securing a better financial base for in-service training.

In addition, he deserves a grade A for not being afraid of offending his own party (but then he was not afraid of offending anybody else, so why should his party be exempt?), for his considerable industry, because anyone who reads every HMI report is either an incorrigible masochist or first in line for the next George Cross, and for his flexibility, as evidenced by his rejection of a parents' majority on governing bodies, or the linking of teachers' pay and assessment, in the light of negative reactions.

The debit side of his profile records how he failed monumentally on something he himself always valued highly, the ability to manage his fellow human beings. Many heads, administrators and teachers are sad that he allowed that precious commodity, goodwill, to evaporate. Goodwill in schools is a little bit like the helium in a balloon, invisible and taken for granted. It is only when it is removed that you realize what he did. For demolishing it, something even the most cretinous and ham-fisted of his predecessors had failed to do, Sir Keith must be given E quintuple minus.

The weakness of his less competent twin brother, Sir Monty Python, was of two kinds. The first was a psychological inability to utter soothing words about teachers. I have no idea why this should be. Perhaps he was unkindly treated by teachers in his youth. Was he, one wonders, given a detention for putting tin tacks on the teacher's chair, running a book on the Derby, or smoking behind the bike shed? Hardly. I imagine him as the bright, industrious pupil picking up high grades and eschewing the sort of behaviour that would have brought him up before the beak.

During a radio programme, in which I had chided him for not recognizing the countless good things that teachers accomplished, he said he would like to give more praise, but, if he did so, large numbers of parents would say: 'That man's talking rubbish'. After the recording I promised to send him some examples of good practice which he could use. A few months later I wrote to him giving him details of the notable achievements of teachers, pupils, and indeed parents, in the 12,300 schools that had surveyed the United Kingdom as part of the BBC Domesday Project. I pointed out that it was the most impressive collaborative project by such a partnership anywhere in the world, and he could safely mention it in a speech as a plus for the education system. He never did.

The second kind of ineptitude showed in the many bizarre Crazy Horse stories about his regular eccentricities. Most of them stemmed from his essentially alien status as KJ the benign extra-terrestrial mega-genius, a million light years away from the proletariat in particular. Hence the substantially true stores of conversations with bemused LEA officials ('Are your primary schools really rigorous?'), low-achieving fifth years ('What do you think of integrated humanities?'), or, it is said, with his boiled egg during breakfast. Actually it was probably not a boiled egg at all, but rather his leader Zarg.

Yet each time I met him I liked him more, and it is a pity that most teachers never saw him relaxed and good-humoured. On television he was a nightmare, unhappy, tense, his craggy features etched deeper by the minute with angst. With radio he was more comfortable, though still not entirely at ease. I did four Radio 4 interviews with him in his enormous throne room at the DES. 'Why are parents having to pay so much money towards the basics of education like books, Sir Keith?' Deep dismay. Sir Keith sighs, sinks his head deep into his hands and lapses into a 30-second coma. 'You see . . . the Government . . . the Government . . . just a minute, I'm going to get my syntax wrong . . . are we still rolling? . . .' Another 20 seconds of anguished silence, BBC sound recordist and producer go quietly crazy. It was not his fault, thoughtful man that he is, that the wretched mass medium required a convincing over-simplification of the complex in less than a minute.

Another face that was never seen publicly was the liberal politician defending schools against the intemperate right wing. He once came to address a Saturday meeting of his political supporters in our own lecture theatre. My colleague Professor Richard Pring and I were due to meet him afterwards. As the room filled up with a mixture of solid citizens and the kind of ferocious retired brigadiers who send nervous citizens like me scuttling for cover, Richard and I debated how we might eavesdrop on this momentous event without actually donning false beard and dark glasses.

We decided to tiptoe up the back stairs and hide in the projection room, somewhat undignified for two university professors, but, if rumbled, we could always pretend to be cleaners, or argue that Sir Keith's cuts had forced us to use the attic as our study. The event was marvellous to behold. As one beetroot-faced critic after another sprang up to ask what he proposed to do about all the left-wing teachers fomenting revolution in South-West schools ('Where on earth were they?' we asked ourselves), Sir Keith urged them to produce evidence, not hot air, and defended schools in a way not often witnessed publicly.

I shall want to remember him as a bright, likeable and compassionate man who had the best of intentions. His tendency to invent policy on the hoof could be alarming, but at least he cared a great deal and worked hard at his brief and that must count for something in a world where politicians frequently appear to the public to be indolent and indifferent.

Teachers are the easiest people in the world to work with, and unfortunately it is here that Sir Keith irrevocably and comprehensively blew it. I suspect his successor, Mr Bun the Baker of the smiling spectacles, will reap credit for the angular Sir Keith's groundwork, but I hope history accords Sir Keith some decent measure of recognition too.

He reminds me of the man in the restaurant seen weeping profusely by embarrassed fellow diners. Eventually one plucks up enough courage to ask him why he is so upset.

The man stops sobbing briefly and replies: 'I don't know why, but nobody likes me, fish-face'. If only he could have brought himself to love teachers just a little.

30 May 1986

2

The rise and fall of Mr Bun the Baker

Whereas Sir Keith Joseph had been at the end of his career and so, though keen to do something useful, was not ambitious for high office, Kenneth Baker (1986–89) was the first of a set of go-getters who had designs on the leadership. He was also the first Conservative education minister in this period to work at his personal image in the press and on television. The 1988 Education Act was intended to be his finest hour. Alas, if only he had listened more and strutted less, it might have got off to a better start.

Magic mirror

A few years ago I worked with an intriguing and occasionally irritating mystic. Every piece of work he ever received he awarded exactly the same mark, namely a grade B. Occasionally I would remonstrate with him, pointing out that I had scrutinized the work in question and, in my view, its quality was equivalent to, not to put too fine a point on it, a load of horse droppings.

Thereupon a pained look would flit across his face and he would say something like this: 'It is what you make of it. You the perceiver must make of it what you choose. I will see it as I want to see it, and you in turn will see in it whatever you wish'. It was only when the National Curriculum appeared that I finally understood this magic mirror view of life, for it too seems to be whatever one wishes it to be.

Indeed its outline has become even fuzzier since last summer when the DES consultative paper, *National Curriculum 5-16*, was launched as most people were about to depart for their annual vacation. At that time, you will recall, the version you perused on Benidorm beach or while cantering on the back of a Blackpool donkey postulated 10 per cent sabre-toothed tiger hunting, 20 per cent mammoth skinning, or some such quantified version of life in school.

According to Julian Haviland in *Take Care, Mr Baker!*, his recent book analysing the replies to the DES consultative document, even though most people were in favour in principle of some kind of national guidelines, out of 11,790 people who mentioned the National Curriculum in their response, the British All-Comers' Record of 11,790 expressed reservations about this particular inspired view of the needs of citizens of the twenty-first century.

Now this is where the story gets complicated. Poor old Mr Bun, by nature and instinct an enlightened liberal, was desperately trying to appease the rotating eyeballs faction of his party by making his macho conference speech about ploughing on to the end of the furrow, and, for all I know, straight through the tulip bed, over the front lawn and across the middle of the dining room carpet. At the same time, friend and foe alike were welcoming his National Curriculum with the warmth and affection normally lavished on someone else's pet tarantula.

On the one hand, therefore, he had to appear to change nothing in order to show how tough he could be with that group of people known contemptuously in political circles nowadays as 'the educational establishment', but still referred to in other lands more affectionately as 'teachers'. On the other hand, common sense and informed advice were screaming at him that Plan A was distinctly duff.

Since last autumn the concept of the National Curriculum has become a blob of mercury, rolling formlessly, ever changing, one thing one day, another the next. No longer was it to occupy 80 to 90 per cent of school time, but more like 70 per cent, until junior minister Bob Dunn said in a Commons Committee meeting that it might be 1 per cent or 99 per cent. Clear enough so far?

Next we were told it was to be a framework not a straitjacket. Yet the notorious Clause 9 requires anyone who wishes to vary the National Curriculum to obtain the Secretary of State's personal authorization. So far as I know, even dangerous loonies in high security jails do not have to get a minister's permission to take off their straitjacket, so that particular piece of information was about as helpful as telling us it was a pullover not a carpet slipper, or a plastic bag not a jam jar.

The latest twist is a stroke of sheer unparalleled genius. The relevant buzz-word is 'cross-curricular themes' which was lobbed into the debate early on the grounds that (a) the proposals were probably going to get a pasting for being dominated by single subjects, upsetting primary or TVEI teachers, and (b) it could be a catch-all category for anything that had been forgotten or to see off vociferous lobbies and pressure groups.

Recently, I received a letter from the DES about a conference on health education which, it was said, was going to be, as I was no doubt aware, 'one of the most important cross-curricular themes in the new National Curriculum'. Well, though I am delighted to hear it, I was not aware of this at all. In fact I have been busy complaining that it only got one line in the original consultative paper under the heading of 'biology'.

My colleague Richard Pring met a banker who said how worried he had been that business studies and economic awareness were not featured more prominently. He was now feeling happier, however, because one of his friends had been on a deputation to see Mr Bun who had assured them that they were to be 'one of the most important cross-curricular themes in the new National Curriculum'.

A couple of weeks ago, Mr Bun announced that technology was not going to be a subject as such, nothing so dreary and old-fashioned, but rather pervade every facet of learning, because it would be 'one of the most important cross-curricular themes in the new National Curriculum'. All of which leaves one unanswered question about the National Curriculum: *What the hell is it?*

Just think of the possibilities. Ballroom dancing? No problem. It will be 'one of the most important cross-curricular themes in the new National Curriculum'. So you can safely samba in science, tango in technology (whoops, that's a theme now, I forgot) and boogie in biology.

This is going to be terrific news for my old friends the British Egg Information Service who, you may remember, are frantically trying to get eggs into the curriculum. They tell me in their latest information sheet that they have launched a video (good move, could count as technology) called *Royal Yolk* (clever title, echoes of history across the curriculum) which 'takes the viewer around an egg farm in an amusing way' (go for it, foxtrot round the farmyard and get in on the ballroom dancing lobby), and 'addresses the serious and sometimes emotive issues' of intensive farming (game, set and match; a nice each-way bet this one, either Eggological Sciences as a subject, or Eggs and the Emotions as a cross-curricular theme). Add 'em to the blob of mercury, Ken, they deserve it.

8 April 1988

The proper use of the B-day

It was quite a shock to see my 13-year-old son applying the contents of a tube of Brylcreem to his hair. The first thought to hit me was that I had missed some obscure clause in Mr Bun's Education Act which made slicking back the locks a compulsory component of the National Curriculum for third-years. The whole country would eventually be teeming with millions of beaming clones of Old Smoothie. Just when I had begun to work out the in-service implications of such a move, I discovered the much more innocent explanation was that the gel version of our traditional hair-cream has become popular with trendy adolescents. It was as well that no further demands were to be made on in-service resources, because the implications of the 1988 Education Act will swallow most of the budget for years to come. Forget about doing anything of your choice on the professional front. Learning Bunspeak will be the top priority.

Mr Bun has already announced that there will be a magic number which will apply to in-service programmes. The number two will dominate all. For a start the induction courses will last precisely two days. This is based on the contemptuous notion that any fool can teach, so a couple of days for senior people gives sufficient information.

They can then go back to their colleagues and sprinkle it on them in a couple of hours. This was the pattern which turned out to be so inadequate for the GCSE. It was called the cascade method of training, but some people named it the piston model. If the subtlety of that epithet is not apparent, try saying it with a pause before the last two letters.

I wonder if the magic number two is used by other professions for important new initiatives. Perhaps it is the way heart transplant surgery is taught. Day one: how to remove a person's heart. Day two: how to put someone else's back in so no one will notice. No doubt the engineers do it as well. Day one: how to build a suspension bridge. Day two: how to stick it back up again when it has fallen down.

For those eager to know Mr Bun's plans for these two riveting days, I can reveal that a secret copy of the National Double B-day Festival has fallen into my hands. In in-service patois, Baker Days are known as B-days on the grounds that although everyone knows what they are, no one knows how to use them properly (B-days – bidets, geddit?).

The magic number two dominates everything. The first day begins with 'an explanation of the intellectual reasoning behind the Education Act'.

This lasts two minutes, to allow the speaker to cover the topic twice.

Next we move on to the National Curriculum. Teachers will learn how to teach the two national songs. 'Greensleeves' (primary) and 'Land of Hope and Glory' (secondary), and how to do a literary criticism of the two national poems – both from *Mr Bun's Bumper Funbook of English Verse*, which will be a set book – 'Wee Willie Winkie' (primary) and the clean version of 'The boy stood on the burning deck' (secondary).

In the lit. crit. session there will be an explanation of how 'Wee Willie Winkie' is actually an ode to Government social policy. The

'Willie' was in fact William Whitelaw when he was Home Secretary, touring the inner cities each evening disguised as an enormous marquee looking for candidates who needed a short, sharp shock. Compulsory going-to-bed at eight o'clock comes in the Government's family responsibility programme.

Day one ends with a two-hour session on national testing at 7, 11, 14 and 16. The first hour will show teachers how to draw ticks and crosses and put in detention those with low marks. The second hour is entitled 'How-to-deal-with-angry-and-upset-parents-of-seven-year-olds-who-have-had-many-sleepless-nights-and-wonder-if-their-child-is-a-complete-moron-and-who-thought-up-this-bloody-stupid-notion-anyway'.

Day two covers raising money when your school is bankrupt because it was inadequately resourced under local financial management. This consists of sessions on 'how to organize a raffle', 'the teacher as busker', 'bank robbery for beginners' (including 'which end to saw off your shotgun' for CDT teachers), and 'seven painless methods of suicide'. For schools opting out of local authority control there will be a lecture on what the Government will do to help, entitled 'You're on your own now, matey'.

Two higher degrees can be obtained. Those who attend day one will be awarded the degree of MB (Master of Bunspeak), and completing both days gains the MBA (Master of Bugger All). Where contempt for professional skill and pride is concerned, two days, two hours, two minutes, two degrees, two fingers, what's the difference?

9 September 1988

The farce of the flashlight brigade

There was a distinct sense of gloom among the conference of primary heads I was addressing. They had just heard on the radio that Mr Bun, fresh from his trans-Siberian tour of photo opportunities, had announced in his speech to the Conservative Party conference that he was going to restore traditional teaching to primary schools, whatever that might have meant.

Most seemed afraid that he might be knocking on their school door the next morning, accompanied by his usual posse of photographers, cracking a horsewhip and shouting, 'Chant your tables, you swine'.

I tried to reassure them that, if you want to be Prime Minister, you don't harangue your party conference about the virtues of progressive primary education. Tell them you will restore capital punishment for teachers who don't set daily spelling tests and a standing ovation is assured. Party conference time is a game with its own set of rules and conventions. The primary heads were still inconsolable.

It set me thinking about what a daft and over-simplified debate it had all become. The very word 'traditional' immediately secures knee-jerk reactions. Mutter it to one group and a round of drinks will follow to toast solid British virtues such as industry, determination and thoroughness. Utter it in different company and the jeers will ring in your ears as people assume you are out of date, backward looking and embarrassed to the tips of your sensible shoes.

I reflected on a class of seven-year-olds I had been teaching. Had I been traditional or progressive, or, for that matter, did anyone give a hang? I had told them things, which sounds trad enough, but we had done a fair bit of group work, so perhaps I am a progressive. On the other hand, I had told some of the groups what to do, so I must be a traditional progressive, apart from when they are allowed to discuss the task I have set them with fellow pupils, because at these times I am a progressive traditional.

What the primary heads feared was that Mr Bun would try to import the styles of teaching he had seen in between posing for snapshots in the Soviet Union. It would not be so strange if Comrade Bunski had been over-impressed by the sort of primary school we used to have, in the nineteenth century, since therein lie the roots of his Education Act.

Just in case too much nostalgia for those awful days overwhelms us, perhaps we should recall some of their less happy features. Much of the time young children chanted by heart, slogans and epithets they ill-understood, like the capes and bays from Blackpool to Hong Kong when they knew neither what a cape nor a bay was. It made the "ere we go, 'ere we go' equivalents of modern football crowds sound positively cerebral.

While he was in Russia Mr Bun did, of course, give his own exceptionally traditional lesson, which one journalist told me would have secured E-minus on any teacher appraisal. It was shown on national television news when he was seen declaiming 'The Charge of the Light Brigade' to an utterly poleaxed group of Russian teenagers.

My journalist friend tells me it was one of the rummest events he has seen in his cynical life. Apparently Bunski rushed into this room full of bewildered Russian students and produced, as if by magic, a class set of *Bun's Bumper Funbook of English Verse* which he just happened to have with him.

A hapless DES menial had lugged them across Siberia waiting for the right photo opportunity. He is probably now in hospital suffering from a double hernia. It was as if Gorbachev had descended on some unsuspecting GCSE class at Little Piddlington Comprehensive, put on a record of *Gorby's Greatest Hits* and proceeded to do a Cossack dance for the assembled press.

Suddenly this crazy stranger with the manic smile and glinting glasses was ranting on about a battle at which 600 rode into the valley of death. Here was the embarrassing situation of a son of the nation which, during the Crimean War, sent the Light Cavalry Brigade on one of the most futile charges in military history, reading a poem about it to the descendants of those who had slaughtered them. It had all the ingredients of the bad trad lesson, the oblivious preaching to the uncomprehending.

So why had Bun suddenly gone a bundle on resurrecting what was condemned as a failure by successive nineteenth century critics? Listen carefully to the words of his poem and all becomes clear. Canon to the left of him, Canon to the right of him. There were also a few Nikons, Leicas and Sony television cameras back and front.

4 November 1988

Bringing a Martian down to Earth

Dear Zarg,

It was good to receive your annual letter asking for an update on British education for your anthropological guide to the solar system. As you are the only Martian I know, other than the one who works at the Department of Education and Science writing circulars to schools, I am grateful to you for keeping me up to date on what is happening on other planets and only too happy to answer the many questions in your letter.

You mention the radio programme you heard indistinctly in which someone purporting to be a Government minister said that there was no shortage of teachers and that morale was sky high. You ask if this was a radio play about life earlier this century, or whether it is an example of what we Earth people call 'optimism'.

The distinction may be hard for you to follow, but it was not a radio play, though it was a piece of fiction, and 'optimism' is only one of a number of Earth words that might be used to describe it. I am afraid I cannot answer your other queries about whether or not there are fairies at the bottom of the Minister's garden and if pigs can fly.

There is indeed a paradox, as you point out, in the same Ministers who deny any problems in teacher supply being frantic to enlist teachers from other countries. I think you have confused two quite different news stories when you ask why the Minister is recruiting Great Danes and Rottweilers. This has nothing to do with the Government's policy on school discipline. The Minister has been trying to persuade teachers in Denmark and Germany to come and teach in Britain, so your question about whether or not dogs are being recruited as licensed teachers does not apply, though those that can do tens and units will have a sporting chance.

I had not realized that there was such a teacher shortage on Venus that teachers had to be brought in from Mercury and that they were paid huge transfer fees. You ask whether the teachers from Hong Kong who answer the Government's appeal will be paid a transfer fee or need to have £150,000 in their bank account, in accordance with likely policy towards others granted a full British passport.

I do not know the answer to this, nor to your other question about why teachers are not offered higher salaries in Britain to encourage more people into the profession. Incidentally teachers are not being given food rather than money. When you heard they were paid 'peanuts', this was not to be taken literally, though it is probably only a matter of time.

You are right to express concern, by the way, at the circular your Martian colleague at the DES has just sent round to schools about how much time is being spent on each topic in the National Curriculum. I too have read this circular. The reason it has that page of what you call 'pure gemstones' at the front with clarifications like, 'The term "1988 Act" refers to the 1988 Education Reform Act' is, as you suspect, to help all those imported German teachers who might have thought it was the 1988 Road Traffic or Sewage Act.

I was not aware that someone who wrote a similar circular on Jupiter was sent to Neptune for it, but I share your anxiety about asking schools who do topics like 'volcanoes' or 'our village' to fill in hundreds of little squares saying how many hours and minutes of it were mathematics, geography or music. It does not mean that teachers will actually have to sing the National Curriculum, as I gather they do on Uranus, but your expression 'unnecessary bureaucratic bull dung' is near enough to the usual Earth term.

Finally I greatly enjoyed your interpretation of several news stories. I had indeed spotted the national newspaper adverts for the first British astronaut. It is quite true that the person chosen would have to go to Moscow and learn Russian. I had not realized, until you pointed it out, however, that it solved the mystery about Kenneth Baker's political future.

It was all so obvious, when you explained it. The project is being sponsored by television companies, so there will be plenty of photo opportunities, and he will be able to declaim in outer space 'The Charge of the Light Brigade', and other poems from his *Bumper Funbook of English verse*, to his fellow students.

It was your last observation, however, which made it so brilliant, when you revealed that he had already made appointments on other planets, to recruit Martian, Venusian and Neptunian teachers as he slicks his way across the galaxy. 'Vorsprung Durch Brylcreem' as they say on Pluto. Have a good summer.

14 July 1989

Suckers for snake oil hokum

If there is one element of this marketing mad world for which I have had not the smallest grain of sympathy, it is the quest for a corporate image. Commercial outfits are spending vast fortunes on logos, brand images, and choosing 'house colours' as they are called.

The new chief executive of an international hotel chain once decided that their traditional colours of green and white were now dated. He made them change to the colours coffee and cream instead.

Throughout the world hotel signs, sheets, towels, menu cards, letter-heads were scrapped and replaced in the new house colours. Soon afterwards the next supremo made them all switch back to green and white.

All this cavorting and wasting of money in commerce would just be an hilarious aside were it not for the sad fact that education itself, still under the influence of Mr Bun, the supreme after-image, is falling for the hokum of the snake oil vendors. Frantically seeking that elusive corporate image, several institutions of higher education are spending in some cases sums of £30,000 to £50,000 for a logo. The ones I have seen so far include what looks like a broken chess piece, a line with a dot under it, a capital letter and a squashed fried egg.

All I can say is that I am available immediately to any university or polytechnic seeking such a logo. You want a capital letter? I'm your man. I have a choice of twenty-six available in a variety of colours. Anyone wishing to remain anonymous should just send the readies in used notes in a brown envelope, using the pseudonym 'sucker' at this stage.

The bad news is that schools are under pressure to squander their hard earned cash on image-making. A few will no doubt scrap perfectly good school badges in favour of some ludicrously expensive and tasteless example of late twentieth century commercial heraldry. Yet if there is one area where the reality is much more important than the image it is education.

I was wrong incidentally in guessing that Bun would choose a baked bean as the Tory Party's new logo. Instead it was again the torch rampant, but this time one that looked to be moving, with much more prominent licking flames, symbolic, presumably of his management of the education system and the fact that, having torched it, he ran like hell.

You can display a logo on the main street of Salzburg so long as it is made of wrought iron. Even the famous fast food hamburger joint was not allowed to have its customary red and yellow sign but had to settle for a wrought iron bun instead. I must remember to ask them to send one to Baker.

Recently two things happened which cheered me enormously about the complete dedication of the teaching profession. The first was a report from the *Yorkshire Evening Post* about 'the crazed gunman at the centre of a nationwide police hunt'.

Apparently this masked figure with a shotgun kidnapped an official of the National Union of Teachers, shutting him in the boot of his own car and driving off with him.

Could this have been Bun's last desperate act to solve the teacher shortages in some parts of the country by kidnapping citizens and then returning them as licensed teachers elsewhere? But the intrepid NUT man managed to escape and get back home. *The Yorkshire Evening Post* recorded for posterity the utter commitment of Britain's teachers: 'He got help at the first house he came to and, when he arrived home, his teacher wife, who had been working at her desk, had not even noticed he had been missing'. I bet the NUT man had been marking essays in the car boot as well.

Even more cheering was the discovery that the Prime Minister thinks teachers have done well with the GCSE. I actually got this one from the horse's mouth, if you'll forgive the expression, when I met her recently. Not that we often socialize, say at the supermarket checkout, or at the garden centre where she has her hair done. We don't go round together much, well, only rarely. All right, we've just met this once.

The experience reminded me of the quiz game question 'Which famous person once came third in a Charlie Chaplin look-alike competition in Monte Carlo?' The answer is – Charlie Chaplin. Apparently the great man put on his gear, went along to the competition and really did come third. On meeting Miss Piggy, I wondered which of the impressionists had turned up. Full marks for the hair, but ring us again when you've got the voice right.

'What do you think of the GCSE?' she began, so I went into enthusiastic auto-pilot about 'due reward for the sterling efforts of teachers and children', 'a real improvement not an artefact'. Her response was a surprise: 'Oh good, I'm so glad to hear it and I do so agree with you'. So I took the opportunity to say she had been 'a bit naughty' for blocking the proposed A-level reforms. 'But we mustn't change A-level you know', 'Oh yes, we must'. Great fun this, especially as, unlike Bun, I did not have to dive under the table for fear of being fired or handbagged.

On the National Curriculum history 'Plato to NATO' syllabus she was more predictable: '*I don't like* the proposals, *I don't like* them, *I don't like* them at all'. I resisted the temptation to reply: 'So would you say, on balance, that you weren't in favour of them, then?'

Unfortunately I never got round to the spoof conversation I had dreamed up on my way to the tea party: 'I say, I say, I say, Miss Piggy, do you know how to get children through the National Curriculum in one third of the time?' 'No, my good man, do tell me' 'Microwave them'. I meant to, but I forgot. Another CBE down the drain.

20 October 1989

3

Genghis Ken the Second

After a brief interlude with John MacGregor (1989–90) as Minister, a man who did actually try to listen to professional advice, the second Tarzan of the day, Kenneth Clarke (1990–1992), made his appearance. Most of the high profile business had been picked over by his predecessor, so he was left trying to find an issue on which to hang his hat. Putting the boot into teacher training and Her Majesty's Inspectorate was amongst the few ways of notching up brownie points with the powerful right-wing, so that is what he did. I was not surprised when he later admitted he had not read the Maastricht Treaty. Reading was never his long suit when he was in the Department of Education and Science.

Of mad dogs and education ministers . . .

Have you heard the story about the world's most intelligent dog competition – staged to find the most intelligent dog in the world? Three finalists appeared with their proud owners and paraded up and down before the most senior judge in the world, seated at a table bearing a magnificent gleaming silver championship trophy.

The distinguished judge stood up and announced to the huge audience the details of the final and decisive test the dogs would have to complete. The three dogs and their owners, an engineer, a sculptor and a government minister, listened attentively as the judge explained that a hundred bones would be laid on the floor. Whichever dog assembled these into the most interesting and complex construction would win the priceless silver trophy and the title of 'Most Intelligent Dog in the World'.

The first competitor, the engineer, stepped forward. 'Brunel, Brunel, go boy', he called, and the dog immediately raced into the arena, scuttled hither and thither among the bones, and assembled the most intricate model of a suspension bridge. The crowd thundered applause and the judge, seated at his table, made copious approving notes.

Next the sculptor strode into the ring. 'Epstein, Epstein, go boy', he yelled, and the second eager dog raced over to the pile of bones and fashioned an incredibly lifelike head and shoulders bust of Beethoven. There were gasps from the crowd. Surely the silver trophy had already been won.

Finally the government minister came forward. 'Bullshit, Bullshit, go boy', he called, whereupon the third dog strolled into the arena, ate all the bones, bit the judge, widdled on the table leg, picked up the trophy and went home for the rest of the day.

I tell this story not merely as a roundabout way of saying all government ministers are superficial, opportunist, contemptuous and indolent, because although some are, others are industrious, concerned and self-effacing, but rather because I am perplexed about the behaviour of some education ministers of late.

Our ministers tend to get a relatively short time in office, though it is not as bad as in some countries. Although being Secretary of State is a high-profile job, being a junior minister can have as much impact as a speck of snow landing on Alaska. Remember Joe Thing and Harry Whatsit, or was it Joe Whatsit and Harry Thing? No? Neither do I. The more forgettable did their greatest service to education when they resigned.

I have been racking my brains to work out what is afoot with our current crop of ministers. During the extensive debates on the 1944 Education Act, R.A. Butler was at pains to point out that he had no intention of interfering in the school curriculum. This promise was repeated, though with much less conviction, by Kenneth Baker when the 1988 Act was going through Parliament. He pointed out that schools would be cushioned from political interference by various councils for curriculum and examinations.

So why then is Mr Clarke laying down the law about the content of geography, history or any other subject? Why does a politician decide, for example, the place of skills in a subject like geography, saying that there is less need for these since they are taught in other subjects? Fair enough, I suppose. I often do mapping in my music lessons.

I can now reveal the true purpose of much recent ministerial behaviour, and it is this. I know you will find this hard to believe, but the reason is that *ministers intend to teach the National Curriculum themselves*.

Shocked? I thought you might be, but look at the evidence. A couple of weeks ago junior minister Michael Fallon, a member of the No Turning Up Group, produced a league table of all local authorities, ranked according to their exam results at 16 plus.

This was said by many to be a cheap political trick, because, as everyone knows, social class correlates highly with exam success, so those authorities with more socially privileged children, often in Conservative areas, will usually outscore those in depressed areas, which are often Labour-controlled. Only fools take these unadjusted league tables seriously and Professor John Gray of Sheffield University has shown that if you partial out the social class element the picture changes dramatically.

However, I can reveal that good old Mike's real purpose in this exercise was to teach maths National Curriculum attainment target nine (using and applying mathematics), level seven, which states, 'follow a chain of mathematical reasoning, spotting inconsistencies . . . make a collection of graphs or charts from daily newspapers;

consider whether any of them are misleading'. Thanks Mike, nice lesson plan.

Then there was Mr Clarke at the North of England Conference, playing his Genghis Ken role as the thinking man's thug. He managed to get a round of booing when asked about the bribes he was offering to schools to opt out by suggesting that, if the audience thought the Government would soon stop the hand-outs once they had most schools in their grasp, they should get their application in quickly. That was design and technology attainment target four (appraising), level four: 'Review the judgements they have made in achieving their final artefacts.'

On this shabby opting-out issue, it was the parents of Devon's King Edward VI School, Totnes, who did the best National Curriculum implementation. Despite all ministerial offers, they produced their own booklet entitled, 'No thank you, Mr Clarke', and then sensibly voted by an overwhelming majority against opting out. This fulfilled history attainment target three (acquiring and evaluating historical information), level three,' 'reorganize and comment on the amount of information provided by different sources . . . recognize fictional aspects . . . gross exaggeration of the achievement . . . or distortion'. Nice one, parents.

8 February 1991

The brat sat on the mat

Tim and His Tests: a new graded reading scheme for primary schools

Book 1:
Tim had a test. It was called a SAT. He got it from Ken. Tim and Ken are men. Tim likes his test. 'My test is best,' says Tim. 'Tim has a good test,' says Ken, 'I like his test. It is the best.' Ken likes a pub. He likes his grub. He likes grub in a pub. But he likes Tim's test the best. 'Rub a dub dub. I like grub in a pub,' says Ken, 'but Tim's test is the best.'

Book 2:

Pat is a head. Matt is a head. Nat is a head. They are all heads. Pat is mad. She is very mad. She is very, very mad. 'Tim's test is bad,' says Pat. 'I am sad,' says Matt. 'Tim is a bad cad,' says Nat. 'Tim is a bad, bad, lad,' says Pat. 'His test is a fad'. 'I will tell his dad,' says Matt, 'Tim and Ken are mad, bad lads.' 'By gad, I am sad,' says Nat. Pat, Matt and Nat are all sad heads.

Book 3:

Tim's test is a SAT. It takes a long time. Pat is in her prime. 'Tim's test is slime,' says Pat, 'It is not worth a dime,' 'My test is fine,' says Tim. 'Do not pine. I must draw the line.' 'Then draw the line fine,' says Matt, 'under your SAT.' 'Put your SAT under your mat,' says Nat, 'Or give it to the cat.' 'Please do not whine,' says Tim. 'My SAT is fine. What's more, it's all mine.' 'The heads do not shine,' says Ken. 'I like wine from the vine when I dine in the pub.'

Book 4:

Pat, Matt and Nat were once like a lat. But now they get fat. They used to drink shorts, but now they drink vats. 'Tim's SAT is tat,' said Pat, 'and he is a brat.' 'Ken is a prat,' said Matt.

'What did you do with your SAT?' asked Nat. 'I hit my SAT with a bat,' said Pat. 'I sat on my SAT,' said Matt. 'I shat on my SAT,' said Nat. Nat was rude. He was a rude dude. He wanted to be rude to Ken and Tim, so he was hoping to be elected president of the National Association of Headteachers one day.

Book 5:

'Bong, bong,' said Pat, hitting Tim with a gong. 'Your test is too long. It has a pong and it is wrong.' 'My test is not too long,' said Tim. 'It is just right.' 'It is not bright,' said Matt, 'it gave me a fright. Don't be so tight.' 'Talk to a kid,' said Nat, 'Then you'll get rid.'

Tim talked to three kids. 'I'm level 1. I'm thick,' said Dick. 'I'm level 2. I'm slick,' said Nick. 'I'm level 3. I'm sick,' said Marmaduke Ffrench-Fitzwarren, 'but that's because my parents assiduously bought all the set books, made me learn them off by heart and what is more, paid several thousand pounds for a private tutor – and I was rather hoping to be level 4, but what do you expect in this regrettably egalitarian age?'

Book 6:

'I've got an idea,' said Tim to Ken. 'I wish I had an idea,' said Ken to Tim. 'Can I have your idea?' 'No you can't,' said Tim crossly, 'It's my idea. I though of it first.' 'All right,' said Ken. 'Tell me your idea and then we'll have some grub in the pub.'

'Well, you know how the SAT took up half a term,' said Tim. 'Did it?' said Ken, 'By the way, what's a SAT?' 'Don't worry,' said Tim, 'you're better off not knowing. Anyway, I'm going to say that it was the teachers' own fault, because they wanted this kind of test.'

'I thought it was your test,' said Ken. 'No, it was really supposed to be your test,' said Tim, 'but we won't go into all that now. Look, I'm going to tell the teachers it will be easier next year. I'll make it last a whole term instead.'

'But isn't a whole term longer than a half term?' asked Ken. 'Yes, of course it is,' replied Tim. 'So won't that make it . . .,' he paused for about half an hour counting first on his fingers and then on his toes, '. . . about three times as long?' 'Twice as long actually,' said Tim. 'So won't teachers have to be pretty silly to believe that it's going to be any better next year then?' asked Ken. 'Very silly indeed,' said Tim.

'Let's go to the pub for some grub,' said Ken. 'Let's eat the same amount of grub, but take twice as long over it. That way we'll get slim,' said Tim. 'You're a clever begger, Eggar,' said Ken.

A real book:

'Where a pupil is unable to complete a SAT due to his absence from school . . . if in the opinion of his headteacher he has not done enough work as aforesaid, the levels of attainment determined by the teacher assessment shall be the levels for the purpose of article 7 unless the local education authority (in the case of a pupil at a school which the authority maintain) or SEAC (in the case of a pupil at a grant-maintained school) disagree, in which case the levels of attainment shall be such as the local authority or SEAC determine by reference to the work the pupil has done on the SAT in question.'

From *The Education (National Curriculum) (Assessment Arrangements in English, Mathematics and Science) (Key Stage 1) Order*, a document sent to all LEAs and other organizations by the Department of Education and Science to clarify the forms of assessment of seven-year-olds in the three core subjects, and also in technology, in 1992.

14 June 1991

Ton-up Clarkie leaves the rest gasping

It is a sign of the times, perhaps, that a great deal of press coverage has been devoted to a group of joyriders who operate at high speed, sometimes doing more than 100 miles per hour, performing regularly in front of crowds of admirers gathered to watch their hair-raising antics. There appears to be little the police can do about them, and some have become media characters, bragging to reporters that no one can stop them.

I refer, of course, to that band of ministers who spin off improbable yarns at such incredible velocity that few can catch up with them. Dubbed 'whoppers' by the newspapers, they tell their big ones at speeds way in excess of the national limits as they scorch round the estate where they live – 'The House' as it is known locally – astonishing members at their audacity. A man claiming to be their spokesman, known simply as 'Clarkie', boasted: 'They can't get near us. I often come up with something so daft I have to laugh myself, but by the time someone has spotted it I'm off the estate, doing a ton again.'

'Clarkie' has explained to the press some of the jargon that has grown up around this late-twentieth century phenomenon. The best known technique is 'ram raiding'.

This involves one minister telling a bit of a porky, and then another storming over the top with an absolute whopper. Clarkie often works as a twosome with his mate, nicknamed 'Egger', according to others on the estate, either because he eggs Clarkie on to higher speeds and more dangerous stunts, or because he overeggs the cake.

Vrooooom! 'There has been wide praise from teachers for the SATs . . . teacher friendly . . . the broad lines are OK," said Egger to the National Association of Head Teachers in June. Peeeeeeow! The only complaints came from a few dissidents in the National Union of Teachers, scorched Clarkie, hurling himself suicidally, Evel Knievel style, in his supercharged turbo, over the top of 20 London buses. Both usually wear ski masks – not that anyone has noticed.

Then there is the 'handbrake turn' – a dangerous manoeuvre that involves going at very high speed in one direction and suddenly applying the handbrake so you make a 180-degree turn into reverse. Zoooooom! There is no preferential financial treatment for grant-maintained schools when they opt out of local authority control, claimed Clarkie at the North of England Conference in January. Indeed it was extremely naughty to talk about 'bribery'.

But, a few months later – Screeeech! Look out! Here comes 'Major', the Mr Big of the whoppers, doing a sensational handbrake turn in a letter to the NUT last month: 'We have made no secret of the fact that grant-maintained schools get preferential treatment in allocating grants to capital expenditure. We look favourably at grant-maintained schools to encourage growth of the sector, and I am delighted to see numbers are continuing to grow rapidly.' My dictionary defines bribery as 'money offered to procure action or decision in favour of the giver'. Spot on, squire.

Next there is the 'screamer'. This occurs when one of the whoppers hurtles through at such breathtaking velocity that he is out of sight before anyone can say, 'What the hell. . . .' Again one of the top practitioners of this frenetic art is the ubiquitous Clarkie, who actually said at a press conference about the privatization of the school inspection service: 'Anyone can inspect a school.' 'Would this include certified loonies, chimpanzees and Al Capone, one wanted to ask, but too late. A puff of cigar smoke, a faint whiff of draught lager, and Clarkie was light years away.

Occasionally whoppers will provide some comic relief for the spectators and send out 'Big Mike' Fallon in his baggy costume to ride around on a clapped-out motor scooter at about three miles an hour, sounding off about how *EastEnders* is ruining the nation's youth, clippety clop, clippety clop. It is a bit like Nigel Mansell and Ayrton Senna having a little race on kiddies' trikes – you know they can go at 200 miles per hour round Monza if they want to, but, good sports that they are, anything for a laugh.

One of the more impressive pieces of comic relief again came from Clarkie, in holiday mood. When asked why the Government was removing subsidies from non-vocational adult education, which would mean that fees would be trebled or quadrupled, and probably kill it off altogether for many people, he said that he did not see why public money should be spent subsidizing evening classes for wealthy old-age pensioners in his constituency, which is a rather humorous view of a move that may well end adult and community education for hundreds of thousands of needy people. Clippety clop, clippety clop. Send in the clowns.

One of the most amazing techniques is the 'sound of silence'. Here the whopper says nothing at all. Clarkie was again peerless when he appeared before a parliamentary select committee and claimed there was nothing he could do to improve standards of reading, as he was not really in charge. Yet he controls the curriculum, the testing, the cash, the salaries and conditions of teachers, was able to dispense with the heads of the National Curriculum Council and the School Examinations and Assessment Council at little notice, and acquired more than 400 extra powers under the 1988 Education Act.

There was no profound comment when it was revealed that a school had taken on an 18-year-old lad as a teacher at £8,500 a year.

But the whoppers have been revving up for a couple of years, saying there is no teacher shortage (although still investing a couple of million pounds in a recruiting campaign for an apparently non-existent problem) and endorsing the shabby licensed teacher scheme. Roll up, roll up, only one year of higher education necessary. Roll up, roll up, no years at all. (My son has just finished his GCSEs. Any offers?)

There was no perceptible rush through the sound barrier on this one. Stand back and applaud the breathtaking audacity of it all.

20 September 1991

Gouda man slams in the lamb

A butcher can inspect a school. Yes, it's official. Recently Kenneth Clarke was asked if, given that he thought anyone could inspect a school, a butcher might one day perform the honours. Our estimable Secretary of State duly confirmed that a butcher could indeed wield his chopper on the educational system. Her Majesty's Inspectorate is at this moment writing its latest masterpiece, *A Butcher's Guide to School Inspection*, published by HMSO at £29.95 (or loose, £9.95 a pound).

I look forward to the meat purveyor's perspective on such matters as whether or not the teacher is using a suitable language register, or giving appropriate practical experience, when explaining concepts to children with learning difficulties, or 'pupils at the scrag end of the educational system', as they will no doubt be known. I can hardly wait for a verdict on cross-curricular themes in the National Curriculum, the very steak and kidney pie of primary education, or what to do with disruptive adolescents. Let us not mince words, sausages, it's absolutely offal. Veal hate it.

You may well wonder what on earth press conferences are like if you have only seen one on television. Kenneth Clarke tends to sit there like a big slab of Gouda, effortlessly churning out the clichés, confirming the Prime Minister's shrewd selection of him to bland for Britain in the forthcoming World Hackney Championships sponsored by Bromide. Since the Big Cheese is currently on a wheeze-a-week campaign in the run-up to an election, these platitude-laden press conferences seem to take place all the time, usually in front of the Department of Education and Science logo, under the slogan, 'If you're in a mess, phone the DES'. If case you missed the last one, here is a transcript.

'Ladies and gentlemen, welcome to my latest press conference in which I shall be announcing some important developments in primary education. First of all let me say something about the testing of seven-year-olds. You will note from the 600 page press release that I have changed some of the set books since last year. We have decided to drop *Little Twinky Smokes Pot* and replace it with *Little Twinky Becomes a Stockbroker*. Teachers will require children to read 100 words from a set text and since it was pointed out last year that *Little Twinky Buys his Council Flat* was only 91 words long, I have instructed teachers to make them read the words inside the back cover as well: 'All rights reserved London and New York. Vote Conservative.'

'Next I want to tell you about the inquiry I am setting up into primary teaching. This will be a far-reaching study and will report next Tuesday. I have given the committee a free hand with no government interference, to find out why primary schools are such a shambles. Objective background information will be brought to the committee's attention to focus its thinking, like the excellent research conducted by Colonel Adam Smith-Rightwinger into primary teachers, *They're all Marxists, the bastards.*'

'The brief includes fundamental, but open questions such as: 'Should children be streamed at birth?' and 'Why oh why is topic and project work such a waste of time, when we never did it at my public school and I can't say that's ever been a handicap to me?' There is the supplementary question the committee will address:

'Shall we make children sit in rows from January onwards, or will it take a few weeks longer to sell off all the tables and buy some decent desks?'

'I should like to deny most strenuously the accusation from my critics that I simply hanker after the past and wish to restore what went on in previous centuries. Verily that is most disagreeable. I hold ye teacher in ye highest regard, i' faith. To him who speaks ill of me I say, 'Hist, mongrel grim, thou know'st me not.' It would be rather nice to hear ye 12 times table being chanted again though. Now, any questions, varlets?'

'*Anne Scroggins,* Daily Globe. *Mr Clarke, I have managed to obtain a copy of the letter you have written to the members of this primary inquiry committee, in which you say: "I am writing to ask you to serve on a committee of inquiry into primary education. Please bring your own hatchet to the first meeting. PS: Really put the boot in, lads, or you'll all be singing soprano." Would you like to comment on that?'*

'I repeat what I have already said. The committee will be entirely free to write its report in my own words. Next question.'

'*Bill Ponsonby,* Sunday Bugle. *Mr Clarke, is it true that what you know about education could be written down on the back of a postage stamp and still leave enough room for a couple of verses of "Rule Britannia"? And that you never answer journalists' questions properly because you are so ignorant about what is happening?'*

'Let me repeat what I have already said. Labour councils and the teacher unions have ruined primary schools. Yes, chap at the back in grey suit and glasses.'

'*John Major,* Prime Minister's Gazette. *Mr Clarke, would you repeat after me the following words: "I will do exactly what I am told if I want to stay in the Cabinet"?'*

'I will do exactly what I am told if I want to stay in the Cabinet. Yes, next question, man at the back in the blue-and-white striped apron with the big basket.'

'*Dewhurst,* Butchers' Monthly. *Mr Clarke, I don't really understand any of this. Can you explain to me exactly what they do in primary schools?'*

'Ah, can I have a couple of pork chops please, and some of that nice lamb? Would you mind inspecting a school for me before you go? You wouldn't like to be on my primary committee by any chance, would you? Don't forget to bring your cleaver.'

13 December 1991

Descartes thinks but Clarke Disney

The news that several teachers had applied for jobs with Euro-Disney in France was depressing, especially when some said they did not care what job they took so long as they could escape, but it did not surprise me. It was probably the best chance they would ever get to present Mickey Mouse with a Kenneth Clarke watch – no hands, just two fingers pointing at the nearest school. Imagine arriving in Paris and finding that Clarkie and Michael Fallon had landed the plum jobs as Donald Duck and Goofy.

I nearly joined them myself when I read that Kenneth Clarke had been described by a colleague as 'one of the party's deeper thinkers'. *One of the party's deeper thinkers?* We are talking huge national emergencies here. Dial 999 immediately. Ask for the whole lot – police, ambulance, fire brigade, 7th Tank Regiment. If Clarkie is the party's Plato, then please, Euro-Disney, hire me immediately as a chipmunk, Snow White, anything, before I meet the party's Pluto.

Take the National Curriculum, for example, What is desperately needed here is partly better thinking, partly better management. Anyone with more than 10 brain cells, Plato or Pluto, can see that it has become exactly what was predicted: a nightmare of 10 discrete, overly prescriptive, separately conceived subjects, rather than an intelligent framework for an organic whole curriculum. A real thinker and manager would find a way of making the enterprise simpler, clearer, challenging, but feasible.

Back in late July 1987, when Kenneth Baker began a lengthy consultation process that was to last well into the following week, some 11,790 people wrote in to offer their comments on the proposed National Curriculum. Many were in favour of a central core, but, according to Julian Haviland, who read all the replies and then summarized them in his book *Take Care, Mr Baker!*, precisely 11,790 out of 11,790 were against what was being proposed. This must still be the British, Commonwealth, European, World and Inter-galactic record for fore-warning.

Unfortunately Kenneth Baker, star of the Hollywood blockbuster *Jungle Macho Guy* ('Me future leader [pounds chest], me plough on to end of furrow, me no deviate under any circumstances from crappy plan') ignored all the unambiguous advice about the folly of locking

10 different groups of subject enthusiasts in 10 different rooms for several weeks. Everyone else knew that what they collectively produced would not cohere and would probably add up to at least 200 per cent of the week.

In theory there was a way out, as the National Curriculum Council would later make sense of disparate and possibly self-contradictory proposals. Had John MacGregor, the only real ministerial thinker and manager in recent years, stayed at the DES, this two-tier strategy would have worked. Unfortunately the next Hollywood blockbuster saw the screen debut of Kenneth Clarke in *Jungle Macho Guy 2* ('Me future leader [tries to pound chest, has difficulty finding it, eventually swings fist, but misses], me plough on to end of six-pack, me deep-thinking Greek philosopher Pluto'), and the whole Silly Symphony then became political, more about power and control than sense.

The problem is that the first sifting of National Curriculum documents was usually done by right-wing pressure groups, whose pronouncements were given more prominence in the press, and taken much more seriously by ministers, than the original reports. So English was supposed to have no grammar or structure, history no facts, and music was all reggae and no Mozart. The truth of the matter is that Brian Cox, chairman of the English working party, has had to write his own book to put the record straight (*Cox on Cox*, a very good, if disturbing, read), and the history syllabus is dripping with knowledge spread over five millennia. Many of our best classical musicians wrote to John Major saying they *liked* the music report and did not want children spending half their time learning how to spell Beethoven, instead of composing and performing.

Were Kenneth Clarke really a good thinker and manager, he would now get the National Curriculum reduced to a single pamphlet, as in most other countries, introduce some flexibility and imagination, and abandon the empty rhetoric about teachers being trendy progressives who do not believe that children should know anything. Instead he neither thinks nor manages. His 'thinking' is confined to stating the blindingly obvious, like saying that trainee teachers should be able to control a class, as if no one had ever thought of it before. Not exactly Immanuel Kant.

His 'management' consists of flooding schools with more and more changes, and then having the cheek to berate teachers, in a television interview, for being unwilling to face up to change, as if there were only one or two minor amendments to cope with.

It is customary to say that people with Clarkie's penchant for management could not manage a whelk stall. But have you ever wondered what would happen if he really did apply the management philosophy he employs with teachers and the National Curriculum to the proverbial whelk stall?

Just imagine you are working behind the counter of the great thinker's whelk stall, 'Arry Stottle's Mucho Macho Whelk Emporium'. The first thing he would do is deliver 20 tons of whelks. Before you had time to unpack them, 50 tons of mussels, 60 tons of periwinkles and 70 tons of cockles would arrive. By now up to your ears in marine gastropods, you would just be able to see 100 pantechnicons pulling in to drop off loads of cabbages, lettuce and tomatoes.

As you disappear from view, smothered, unable to find a single bloody whelk, let alone sell anybody one, consoled only by the thought that, with Baker and Clarke in charge, there will be no need to order oil and vinegar for the salad dressing, you are dimly aware of the great philosopher telling the press the usual Kant: it is all your fault and you will have to stop being a trendy whelk-seller. If Euro-Disney is looking for a really deep thinker to play the part of Dopey, then Kenneth Clarke, the Ludwig Wittgenstein of Westminster, must be their man.

7 February 1992

In a right-wing land, Arbut is king

The right-wing now has an almost complete stranglehold on the education system. Little by little, vacancy by vacancy. Bill by Bill, the Right has occasionally slid, often raced, into an unchallenged position of power and influence. That it should have captured control by protesting over the imagined potency of an 'educational establishment' consisting of teachers, academics, inspectors and civil servants, is but one of a host of ironies and paradoxes that surround this astonishing phenomenon. Its ultimate vision, not too far away now, is 26,000 isolated schools or 'businesses', no HM Inspectorate, no teacher-training institutions, no local authorities, no unions preferably. Just the Government and 26,000 small businesses. A chilling re-creation of the nineteenth century.

Consider the history of the remarkable set of events of the past few years. Before the mid 1980s any proposals to treat education as a street market, with children as cans of own-brand beans, were seen as the gigglesome fantasies of an eccentric fringe. Today they are, following the 1988 Education Act, supreme orthodoxy.

Would anyone have forecast that the people chairing the two major national committees responsible for examinations and curriculum would be removed, and that both their replacements would be from the Number 10 Policy Unit? Or that vacancies on important national committees would unashamedly be filled with people who have not *an* ideology, but *the* ideology? I wonder if Kenneth Clarke rings up John Major, or more likely the other way round, and says, as in the BT advert, 'He's got an Ology'.

Many years ago I knew a man called Arbut, at least, that was his nickname. He was one of the great spotters of paradoxes, ironies, inconsistencies and inaccuracies, and his nickname derived from the habit of saying, 'Ah, but . . .' at the beginning of his observations. Ever since then I have thought of an Arbut as either a unit of measurement of such inconsistencies, or a marker of them. He would have been in his element today.

Most recent legislation has come from ideas produced by right-wing pressure groups. Arbut, is it not the case that these were usually pretty flimsy, ill-researched, often conceived by people without appropriate first-hand experience of classrooms? Schools, it was said, would be liberated from government bureaucracy. Arbut, have they not been buried under vastly more control, form-filling and prescription about curriculum and testing than at any time in our history? A free competitive market would operate between different types of school. Arbut, did not the Government give millions of pounds extra to city technology colleges and grant-maintained schools?

The best Arbuts recently have been in teacher training and the New Zealand-inspired reading recovery scheme.

Kenneth Clarke has proposed that 80 per cent of teacher-training should be based in schools. Arbut, did not a research report by Warwick University show that teachers were already overwhelmed by government demands and were only able to spend a third of their very long working week in the classroom?

Undergraduate BEd training courses should be reduced to three years, analogous to his desire to have two-year university degrees.

Arbut, is not the probationary year about to be abolished and would this not, therefore, reduce a five-year induction phase to just three, putting the profession back to the Fifties and the two-year certificate course, given that the third year would be spent in schools? Does this not come at a time when European countries are strengthening links with higher education, complaining about the shortness of British courses, and when we ourselves are basing nurse training more firmly in higher education, rather than leaving nurses to pick things up on the wards?

I found the announcement about the £3 million for the New Zealand reading scheme hilariously ironic. It was exactly 20 years ago that I had a grant from the Nuffield Foundation for a remedial language programme. We gave more than 100 five-year-olds, in what was then called a social priority school, the English Picture Vocabulary Test and asked each teacher to rate language proficiency on a five-point scale. The lowest achieving quarter was split into experimental and control groups. Each child in the experimental group had individual attention, designed to suit his or her own language needs, for 45 minutes every day from an experienced deputy head given leave for the project.

We delayed six months before following up with tests, to avoid Hawthorne Effect from the excitement of an experiment, but the experimental group won hands down and was, on average, two clear Ladybird readers ahead of the control group. Arbut, was not compensatory education widespread in the 1970s, did not the New Zealand team draw inspiration from good work in Britain and the US, and are they not (wash your mouth out with soap and water) *academics*? Were not both remedial work and teacher release badly damaged by the very cuts in government spending advocated by the right-wing?

Kenneth Clarke is now recruiting a fresh team of advisers, so should you wish to receive an invitation to advise the Government about education. I have obtained from him the six tough new requirements, or 'performance criteria', you will have to meet. You must be able to answer, hand on heart, 'Yes' to *all* the statements below:

I am very, very, very right-wing;
I have not been inside a classroom for years and have no teaching experience;

I think all teachers, academics, inspectors and civil servants are raving Marxists;

I am very, very, very silly;

I can write really silly pamphlets that will have you in absolute tucks before you turn them into legal requirements;

I can rotate one eyeball clockwise and the other anti-clockwise at the same time.

Some of these used to be optional, but they are in future compulsory. If you can answer a truthful 'Yes' to all six, please send a stamped addressed teacher to: Kenneth Clarke, c/o John Major, 'Arbut', Biggotts Welcome, Dunsmilin, Cossit, Herts.

24 January 1992

He came, he saw, he blundered

Not one tear will be shed when Kenneth Clarke empties his desk at the Department of Education and Science for the last time next week. A few would flow if he returned, but even if the Conservatives are re-elected, he will be after some bigger role, Minister of Culture no doubt. I wonder what treasures he will load into his holdall as he departs. An unread copy of the Plowden Report? Dale Carnegie's less well known work *How to Lose Friends and Alienate People?* His *Thesaurus of Insults?*

When he first arrived at the DES someone said he was just the sort of bloke you might meet in a pub. You can meet some very rum coves in a pub and true enough, most of his thoughts on education did have a ring of the saloon bar of the Dog and Duck. 'A pie, a pint, and a platitude' was his motto, not really good enough for someone who, as they used to say before school reports became computerized, could do better.

Eighteen months ago, when he began his term of office, the conditions were very favourable for an incoming minister. The National Curriculum could have been trimmed down to make it workable, bureaucracy was waiting to be reduced, and John MacGregor had swept up some of the odium left by Kenneth Baker. Anyone with energy, wit and good intentions might soon have been the most effective Secretary of State for decades. Instead Kenneth Clarke became master of the effortless cliché, was hissed at virtually every conference he addressed and teachers who were St Francis of Assisi lookalikes turned into foaming psychopaths at the mere mention of his name.

So where did he go wrong? After all, he is clearly not stupid. A former barrister, who had specialized in representing some of the less well off, he should have brought intelligence and empathy to a brief like education. If nothing else the sight of junior minister Big Mike Fallon coming off the subs' bench to warm up should have concentrated his mind.

He promised to reduce bureaucracy, but actually increased it. A couple of weeks ago we received a letter from the DES telling us that he had approved our secondary articled teacher scheme. A week previously we had received another DES missive to say he had decided to end the scheme. In Clarkeland the bureaucracy goes backwards from death to birth, till everything meets at the same point in time and the Universe implodes, the exact opposite of the Big Bang – the Big Squish.

To understand what drove him it is essential to take into account the inescapable fact that he fancied himself as a future Prime Minister, what you might call the Curse of the Ken. Conservative supremos are elected not by the general party membership but by the MPs. This means that aspirant leaders see as their constituency their own mates in Parliament. They have to impress the liberal and reactionary wings of this disparate group. Both Kenneth Baker and Kenneth Clarke felt obliged to talk tough-sounding nonsense, about kicking sense into trendy teachers, in order to appease those who see such pointless thuggery as 'leadership'.

This involved over-simplification of the issues to the point of farce. Anyone disagreeing with him was labelled 'latter-day left-wing apostles of Plowden'. In this grotesquely simple world of stereotypes, teachers were naughty children, parents all agreed with every daft word he uttered, and trouble only occurred in Labour authorities, even though many dedicated Conservative councillors spoke angrily about the way the Government was treating schools and local education authorities.

What was more irritating was his cynical mis-statement of the true state of affairs. He gave the public the impression that a third of seven-year-olds could not read, when this was not the case. Yet here was the one person in the country who could have established exactly what the state of play was, since he had all the resources of the DES at his command.

His insistence that grant-maintained schools were not being offered bribes and his urging of delegates at the North of England Conference to get their bids in quickly if they believed bribes were on offer, won him no respect, especially when John Major later said: 'We have made no secret of the fact that grant-maintained schools get preferential treatment in allocating grants to capital expenditure'.

Now that he is about to go I shall commence work immediately on writing an account of the positive achievements of his 18-month ministry. It will be called *He Came, He Went* and it will be a very short book, well, just the covers and a photograph of him actually, to remind people of what he looked like. In fact, I've finished it already. This very slim work is being published in circular shape, so that it can be opened at his picture and stuck on the staffroom dart board.

I hope that when he finally leaves Sanctuary Buildings, the inappropriately named expensive new headquarters of the DES, unlamented, the deafening cheers of thousands of teachers echoing in his ears, he will quietly obey the instructions on top of his marmalade jar: 'Turn slowly and push off'. In the meantime, I am not often moved to verse, but I have spent several seconds composing this poem dedicated specially to his memory.

So push off, Clarkie.
You plumbed the shallows
Of your mind
A blokey bloke.
'Everything on one sheet of A4'
Was your motto.
Why didn't you read them?

So just push off, Clarkie,
Back to the *Dog and Duck*
Where your thoughts were born.
A pint, a cigar and a Big Mac.
I shall miss you,
Much as I would
Toothache.

3 April 1992

4

Politics, politics

By 1992 John Major had replaced Margaret Thatcher as Prime Minister, and it was clear that Number 10 Downing Street now called the shots where education was concerned. John Patten (1992–94) was another ambitious minister who, like Baker and Clarke, was supposed to be a liberal at heart. You could have fooled me with all of them. Such was the power, by now, of the right-wing over education, that both Patten and Major had to do their bidding. Privatization, league tables, charters, more and more legislation, and a form of competition that was actually rigged in favour of schools sponsored by the Government, became taken-for-granted features of the educational landscape. It was laugh or cry, so I preferred to laugh, and there was plenty that was risible.

Spare us the renting and raving

It has been a fine summer. Teachers returning from a trip abroad a couple of weeks ago must have been reassured to hear that all was fine in education. A beaming John Patten had arranged a photo call one Saturday morning to tell the press that everything was fine. Anyone really relaxed about the state of education would simply have returned to work and got quietly on with it, but old Patters had to summon journalists to photograph him on the lawn holding a cat (or perhaps it was the next junior minister – sleeps all day, comes out at night, but then only to widdle on the back porch).

'How are you feeling Mr Patten?' 'Fine.'
'But didn't things run better in your absence?' 'Fine fine fine.'
'You've just been reshuffled, you're in charge of bus stops.'
'Fine fine fine fine fine.'

Another person confirming how fine education is without him is former junior minister Michael Fallon, who emerged briefly from exile with one of those market-inspired wheezes just like he used to have when he was at the DFE. The latest winner from Big Mike was to suggest that private firms should build and run education buildings and 'education parks', consisting of classrooms, laboratories etc. These would then be rented to higher or further education establishments, maintained or private schools, a move which would 'harness the commercial interest of the private sector'.

It's another belter. I can just see impoverished maintained schools trying to compete for space with richer competitors in the private sector. For the modest rent it could afford, Scumbag Comprehensive would no doubt be offered the chemistry lab on alternate Tuesdays between midnight and 3 a.m. Fine idea. Don't ring us, Mike, we'll ring you.

The inevitable close to the summer nowadays is the publication of the A-level and GCSE results. Last year in the corresponding article to this one, I wrote: 'The saddest spectacle of the summer, however, was the Great Annual Educational Paradox. This is a ritual observed every August when A-level and GCSE results come out. If the results are worse than previously, then it will be said that standards have gone down. If the results are better than the year before, then it will be said that standards have gone down. It is the only aspect of life where both "up" and "down" always mean "down".'

Exactly the same happened again this year. Even though John Patten announced last September that the most stringent marking conditions would be applied in future, and no doubt inspectors have been standing over examiners guiding their hand across the mark sheets, the results were still a percentage point or two up on last year. This did not stop the knee-jerk critics saying it must be a fix. It is about time they gave a bit of grudging credit to the teachers and pupils who are working hard for these improvements.

No summer nowadays would be complete without the innumerable league tables, charts of 'Britain's top schools', parents' guides to the best in private or state schooling, as newspapers and publishers fall over each other to publish what is largely a map of the leafy suburbs. All these places seem to have a head who is a bit of a character, and what is irritating is that nothing ever goes wrong in them. Really? What has happened to all the imperfections we know and love? Is it not time for a guide that tells the whole story?

Poshville Academy

Acacia Villas duplex, Cholmondley-Smythe Avenue, Poshville.

Buildings: Impressive Palladian front conceals crumbling behind, with resplendent gothic dining room, known affectionately to pupils as 'The Cockroachery'.

Head: Oxbridge-educated (Oxbridge secondary modern, Barnsley) Mr I Thrashem rides his motor bike up and down the corridors and engages generally in the sort of certifiable behaviour that would have him trussed safely in a straitjacket anywhere except in this private school.

Academic standards: Quite high average GCSE and A-level points per head, especially as those likely to fail or obtain low grades are not allowed to enter in the first place.

Extra-curricular: Getting out of the school whenever possible, though the head prides himself on the few escapes from Colditz House, the boarders' residence.

Most popular school society: The Olfactory Club, where pupils and staff meet to sniff things.

Uniform: Gold blazers and silly straw boaters. Prefects wear the coveted 'Pre's badge', a cash register rampant over the school motto: 'If they're daft enough to pay, who are we to turn them down?'

Famous former pupils: Marmaduke Cholmondley-Smythe junior, once made 12 not out in a house match.

Michael Fallon Comprehensive
No fixed abode, Somewhere-in-the-Wilderness.
Buildings: Haven't got any, lease ran out on privatized hut.
Head: Joint heads are Botchett and Scarper, Estate Agents, specialists in looking for premises.
Academic standards: Would be good, if only we could find somewhere nice to rent.
Extra-curricular: Since there are no premises, everything is extra-curricular, mainly the Vacant Possession Club which looks for likely squats.
Uniform: Raincoat, sou'wester, umbrella and map. Prefects wear a special badge, a pair of binoculars over a bend sinister bearing the inscription 'To let'. School motto: 'Everything is fine, the free market will solve it – any vacancies by the way?'
Famous former pupils: Cynthia Portakabin.

10 September 1993

Hark, the Patters of tiny pronouncements

Have you noticed the Secretary of State trying to be, well, er, um, er, assertive recently? Yet, it's true, old Patters has been going round stamping his foot like Noddy in a tizz. A drat here, a pish there.

It reminds me of a student teacher a few years ago, who eventually failed her teaching practice because she took no action whatsoever, but just repeated over and over again: 'Now you're all being really, really naughty'.

The first naughty boys and girls were the whole teaching profession for wanting a pay rise. Smack! Slapped wrists all round as strict John sternly pointed out that a pay rise would mean 80,000 redundancies. That's funny. I don't remember judges being fired when they were given a big salary increase. If there is a political will then certain people can be paid more.

It happened with the police and armed forces during another period of pay restraint. A zero salary award is not what John Major talked about when he said he would ensure teachers were well rewarded so they could have a new car in their drive. Now you know what car he meant. It was a Dinky toy.

Drat! The next naughty children were the Oxford University Department of Education for not sending students to do their teaching practice at Eton. 'Now you're being really, really naughty,' said John, stamping his foot angrily, 'and I'll huff and I'll puff and I'll close you right down.' I say, hold on a tick, Patters old bean. Eton is a fine school with a very distinguished tradition. But will the governors of comprehensive schools in big cities welcome someone who trained in a place where there is no obligation to teach the National Curriculum, and where the boys are the children of well-heeled toffs able to shell out £10,000 plus in readies per annum?

Pish! Billy Goat Gruff then set off over the rickety rackety bridge of his shaky policies to find another troll. What better than teacher training and the whole of the teaching profession? It has passed almost unnoticed that yet another shabby and ill thought out 'consultative' (sorry, forgive my mirth) document has been sent round stating that teacher training courses are going to be shortened by a year, and a Teacher Training Agency (agency, for goodness sake; what is this, a profession or a typing pool?) will be set up.

This is another one in the teeth for the teaching profession. First of all by shortening the course to the briefest in Europe it demeans the whole profession. If you can do a degree plus a teacher training qualification in three years, then you have virtually got a two-year degree. Most countries require four, five years or longer.

Secondly, by removing teacher training from mainstream university funding, the message is that medical schools and law schools and every other school will get their funding, just like any other university department, from the Higher Education Funding Council, but education alone will have yet another quango, an agency controlled directly by Patters himself, no doubt with the usual hand-picked squad of trusties, to stop those naughty teachers and teacher trainers stepping out of line.

So why then, after a merciful absence, is old Patters strutting his way through September pretending that people are being really, really naughty, and dratting and pishing at all and sundry? The answer is very simple. September precedes October and it is in October that the party conferences take place. He has to go to his conference knowing that the auditorium is full of people who regard him as a lame duck. So what should he say to them? Quack, quack?

Watch his party conference speech carefully. He will strut and quack, try to sound tough but sensible, and what he says will get a polite ripple of applause at the end of each rising cadence. But the contempt of the audience will be transparent. Many of them are dedicated county councillors who tried to do a good job on their education committee for years then lost their seat in May, partly because of the numerous bog-ups made by Patters, who caused the biggest teacher boycott in history and called parent representatives Neanderthal for their views.

I was reminded of the sheer awfulness of the party conference season when I read Kenneth Baker's much-hyped autobiography *The Turbulent Years*. He was notorious for going along to the conference and making his annual 'I shall plough on to the end of the furrow' speech, thus creating much of the mess that poor old Patters inherited. The bookshop was full of people standing on one leg, skimming the education chapters, so they could read his fanciful account of history without actually adding to his royalties.

Anyone who knows what really happened in education under Baker's stewardship will be amused at the version presented in his book. It was the beginning of the most divisive, chaotic period in education this century, when teachers were buried under the bureaucracy created by his mistrust of them. Yet according to his book he rode up on his white horse, rescued an ungrateful world, put everyone to rights and was the one shining beacon in a sea of incompetence.

Baker is captain of our international smug team and will be preening for Britain in the forthcoming World Self-Satisfaction Championship in Helsinki. His autobiography should have been entitled *Was I Bloody Brilliant, Or Was I Bloody Brilliant?* or *You're All Really, Really Naughty*. This nauseating account states at one point: 'There was only room for one boss in my departments.' More's the pity.

I was just left with one question after reading it. If Kenneth Baker was the Secretary of State who never put a foot wrong, then who was that prat in glasses who made such a mess of things from 1986 to 1990?

24 September 1993

How to sell Patten to the Patagonians

'Do your students have the creative flair to be the business entrepreneurs of the future? If so, we urge you to encourage them to enter Royal Mail International's educational Young Exporter of the Year competition.' Thus runs the opening statement of the latest commercial missive to be sent to schools (three days late if my experience of the Royal Mail is anything to go by).

In order to win a trip to Europe worth £3,000 for five pupils plus the teacher, all they have to do is 'put together a marketing proposal on how they would market a product or service to a named European country'. I suppose it would then be in keeping with the entrepreneurial ethic of the age if the five pupils, having done all the work, were given £50 each to rough it in the Dunkirk youth hostel, while the teacher, acting the 'boss' role, swanned off to the Monte Carlo Hilton. Fortunately teachers are too decent for that.

For anyone interested in entering, I can offer this year's irresistible winning idea. I would export the whole of British education policy, league tables, hit squads, daft bureaucracy, OFSTED, butchers inspecting schools, new curriculum directives every five minutes, bribes for GM schools, silly SATs, Teacher Training Agency and associated 'reforms', Government anthologies of literature, Patten, Blatch, Major, the whole package deal, lock, stock and barrel, to Albania. Brilliant.

Better still, I would export it to all our main business rivals, like Japan, Germany, the United States, and watch them grind remorselessly to a halt under the sheer weight and mindlessness of it all. Then, with the rest of the business world paralysed, we could step in and clean up. Thank you, Royal Mail, for the inspiration.

According to the competition blurb, last year's winners devised a scheme for exporting beer to the Germans. If the idea is to target your marketing on a country that already has a successful product, and persuade them that our own warm and flat equivalent is much better, then this could be even more of a challenge.

We could start by exporting the Government's system of packing committees with their own hand-picked placemen. The idea could be sold to Russia where, since the death of Stalin, this deft skill has fallen into disrepair. The blatant offering of bribes, such as technology projects and new buildings, to schools to induce them to opt out would be much appreciated by the men in dark glasses, expensive suits and black limousines round Naples way. The paper mountain could be relocated in an emormous warehouse somewhere in the European Union.

There are still more superlative ideas to be exported. The young entrepreneurs could think of people abroad they do not like, and then sign them up for John Patten's hazardous 'Truancy Watch' scheme. Even better was his reported plan to make the wearing of school uniform compulsory for all children. Apparently this would help the Truancy Watch people to spot them. 'Mum, I'm just off to play truant and go shoplifting in town.' 'Well make sure you put your school uniform on or you'll get into trouble.'

I am strongly in favour of employing enough educational welfare officers to chase up truants in a proper professional manner, but well-intentioned have-a-go amateurs could experience problems. I can just see the scenario. Officious middle-aged person goes up to spotty youth in record shop: 'Why are you hanging around this record shop instead of attending school today sonny?' 'Because I'm the manager.' Or perhaps: 'Oi, you in the uniform, shouldn't you be somewhere else?' 'Yes madam, I should be piloting a Boeing 747 across the Atlantic, but it's my day off.'

Or alternatively, 'I'm with Truancy Watch, so I want to know why you aren't at school today little boy?' 'I'm helping my dad with the shopping.' 'And which one is your father?' 'He's the big bloke with the tattoos who's just about to put you straight into the intensive care unit.'

If pupils want to export our great education system they will need to create a successful advertising campaign to go with their marketing strategy. There should be no shortage of ideas for the fertile imagination. One obvious inspiration would be the imaginative series of adverts for Hamlet cigars, in which some poor beggar comes to grief and then smokes a cigar to the accompaniment of Bach's *Air on the G string*. John Patten settling down behind the Speaker's chair, having been reprimanded for revealing Education's spending plans four hours before the Budget, curled up in a Union Jack, puffing on a cigar to lugubrious music, would be perfect.

Among numerous other classic advert possibilities would be to nick the Smarties ad of a few years ago. A teacher could be shown sitting behind a huge pile of marking above the slogan 'Wotalotigot'; a crumbling primary school might be portrayed as 'one of the less

fattening centres'; all the hundreds of National Curriculum documents could be seen stacked alongside the legend 'Pure genius'; or
one could filch the wristwatch advert that sums up government policy
to perfection: 'Inspired by the past for the future'.

So get your five pupils together for the Royal Mail competition and
go for it. Let them export bureaucracy to Bulgaria, SATs to San
Salvador, OFSTED up the Orinoco, uniforms to Uruguay, hit squads
to Haiti, league tables to Liberia – and Patten to Patagonia.

17 December 1993

Short back and stupid asides please, John

Ah, at last I've got it. Until last week I did not have a clue what
schools were supposed to do, or how children were supposed to
behave in class. Now, thanks to the Government's 'back to basics'
policy, (or is it 'back to basins', a campaign to restore traditional
haircuts, I'm never quite sure), I finally understand what it is all
about. As John Patten's clichés on discipline hit the broadcasting and
print media like stun grenades, the scales finally fell from the eyes of
430,000 misguided teachers.

It was another successful use of a tactic I encountered as a child
whenever I went to Alf, the local barber. Alf acquired a reputation as
a sage by stating the screamingly self-evident. 'I see it's started to rain
then,' he would observe, as you walked into what passed for a salon
in those days, soaked to the skin. No one ever had the courage to
reply: 'No, you daft brush, I just decided to go for a swim fully
clothed.'

'Looks like United'll be going down,' he would opine a full month
after the end of a season which had seen the local football side finish
10 points adrift at the bottom of the league.

I had never realized that Alf had moved on to become Secretary of
State for Education and had applied the same homespun wisdom to
the great issues of the day until John Patten made his discipline
speech. Schools have 'an enormous responsibility towards the

development of children'. Yes, yes, go for it Alf. Snip, snip, just a bit more off the top please.

'They should not be afraid to teach children to have respect for others and respect for property.' You tell 'em my son. 'Honesty, trust, fairness and self-discipline should be central to schools.' Snip, snip, no hairspray, thanks. Go on sunshine, you're into the home straight now. It's another one in the eye for all those teachers who think dishonesty, mistrust, unfairness and unruliness are better. Back to basins indeed.

What hurts is the constant innuendo, the suggestion that schools do not have rules, so they need the Government to tell them to invent a few. Is there a school anywhere in the country that does not have any rules? Even A.S. Neill's Summerhill, sometimes regarded by the right wing as the supreme example of unruliness, had rules that were drawn up at regular meetings of staff and pupils.

The stage-managed leaks before Patten's speech stated that the Government believed in good behaviour in schools and 'wanted teachers to join them in their campaign'. I'm sorry, Government, would you mind repeating that? I think you may have got it a teeny weeny bit back to front. It is, in fact, teachers who believe in good behaviour. Reports show that most of them ensure it occurs, so they would actually like the Government to join their campaign.

For a positive start, how about a bit of cash to re-employ some of those additional teachers, behaviour specialists, sin-bin operators and educational psychologists whose posts have disappeared because of money shortages? It is not a case, Government, of you being already on the discipline bus, teachers outside. It is more one of teachers actually living on the bus, needing bus fare, Government outside, not giving a toss, except for propaganda value. Get it?

I look forward to the same tactic now being employed in other fields. The Government will no doubt announce before long that it would like the police to stop people committing crimes, and it hopes that the members of the police force 'will join the campaign'. They would also like doctors to cure people who are sick, so they hope that the medical profession 'will join the campaign'. A bit more money for the health service? Sorry squire, it all went in the cuts. Back to basins again, I'm afraid – snip, snip.

The good news is that six circulars with 270 pages of Government 'advice' on discipline are winging their way into schools at this very moment. For those who have not yet seen them, here is a synopsis of the contents:

Bullying: Anyone caught bullying should be kept in after school. Those really good at bullying must be reported to the Government, so they can be given further training as 'persuaders' of parents who are opposed to opting out.

Fairness: Pupils who frequently act in an unfair manner should be sent directly to the Department for Education, where they will be employed as couriers carrying sacks of technology money to schools that opt out.

Smoking: Pupils found smoking are to be punished. In schools sponsored by a tobacco company, they are to be congratulated.

Litter: Dropping litter is not permitted. Children doing so must resign from the school, unless they argue that it is 'a private matter', in which case that is OK by the Prime Minister and most of the Government.

Rewards for good behaviour (pupils): For good work – a star; for ripping off fellow pupils and donating the proceeds to the Government – a knighthood; for being a complete prat – ministerial office; for wanting to be a teacher – ridicule and abuse.

Rewards for good behaviour (teachers): For trying to carry on with the job despite all the aggravation from Government – no pay rise; for working hard to implement the National Curriculum against the odds

– blame for being trendies; for running the school with insufficient cash to do the job – a basinful of basics; for staying in the profession – threats of redundancy; for trying to cope with the demands of the 21st century – the policies and attitudes of the 19th century; for improving exam results – accusations of falling standards; for managing to teach despite diminishing resources – more cuts. Snip, snip.

14 January 1994

Orville and Bean's load of bolero

It's a funny world. Who would ever have thought that it would be possible to become nationally, if not internationally, renowned for simply appearing on television and going round every day uttering mindlessly 'Blobby Blobby Blobby'. Sadly, however, the public seems to have given up expecting any great intellectual stimulation from what he says, so John Major carries on pontificating about education. It is hard to make John Patten look profound, but Major manages it.

In so far as one can work it out, the 'basics' that Major wants to get back to consist of learning to read, write and do sums, and that is as far as it goes, a somewhat unambitious aspiration, hampered apparently by 'the progressives'. In addition, they should also 'learn education'. This must refer to the teacher-training component of a resurrection of his Mum's Army idea. How on earth do children learn education? Presumably in the same way as they eat consumption and breathe respiration. Fred Jarvis, former general secretary of the National Union of Teachers, spent months in correspondence with the Prime Minister desperately trying to find out who these people are who do not believe in children learning to read, write and do sums, but without success. If out of over half a million people who work in education Mr Blobby cannot name one single idiot who is against reading and writing, then he should stop pretending there are such people.

At the same time as I was hearing about the Prime Minister's rudimentary aspirations for education, I happened to be reading an article about the human brain in *Scientific American*. Did you know that the cerebral cortex 'can be subdivided by morphological and functional criteria into numerous sensory receiving areas, motor control areas and less well defined areas in which associative events take place . . . here, in the interface between input and output, the grand syntheses of mental life must occur'? So what goes wrong in the case of Government ministers? Too many 'less well defined areas', I suspect.

Nonetheless, it was a terrific relief to discover that the Government's Back to Basics campaign was nothing at all to do with personal morality, but, as several senior ministers were only too eager to point out, was all about things like education. So that's all right then. Presumably we can now look forward to a massive school building programme.

Here we are six years away from the twenty-first century and surveys show that 85 per cent of schools need building work doing on them, £4 billion is required to put them in order and some school buildings are utterly disgusting. Add to that appalling figure all the people living in cardboard boxes or clapped out housing, mental patients on the streets, large dole queues, huge hospital waiting lists, Dickensian crime rates, filthy overcrowded commuter trains, Victorian hypocrisy, the fact that driving through cities is often slower than in horse-drawn days and a walk on the beach can be like wading through a giant toilet, and we could do with a few basics.

Yet there is no coherent strategy to improve the fabric of education. Major and Patten seem to be the exact opposite of Torvill and Dean. Whereas the ice skating supremos dance as if welded together, Patten rejects nursery education and Major talks of it as a probable election winner. Major tries a triple lutz while Patten pirouettes alone on a different ice rink. It is as if Major is playing table tennis while Patten plays snooker. That analogy is too coherent, however, since both activities are at least games involving a ball. The reality is that Patten would probably be playing table tennis with a snooker cue, while Major used his table tennis bat to play the guitar.

Talking of balls reminds me of one stunning success in the Government's education policy. I have often been critical of the Government, but credit must be given where it is due. I refer to the story of the two 15-year-old pupils who went to a hospital on work experience and then found themselves helping the doctor stitch patients' wounds. It was a triumph not only for Back to Basics, but for the Government's emphasis on children gaining work experience.

Apparently the reason the doctor allowed the 15-year-olds to do some stitching was because he mistakenly thought the two fourth-year pupils on work experience were fourth-year medical students. Only when he tried to engage them in a technical discussion did he realize the mistake.

It is easily done. There must be hundreds of teachers at this very moment being inspected by OFSTED who mistake lay inspectors for the real thing. 'He sat in my lesson making notes and I thought he was a real inspector. It was only when I tried to engage him in a technical discussion afterwards that I realized he was a pensioner on work experience'.

Getting pupils to perform operations is a touch more ambitious than John Major's plan for reading, writing and sums, admittedly, but perhaps, as part of the Back to Basics campaign, the Government will be encouraged to extend the licensed teacher and Mum's Army scheme to the medical profession. After all, if you can stitch on a button, why not have a go at a bit of triple bypass surgery?

Now that the Dearing Committee is opening up the curriculum at key stage 4, I can see all this leading to an exciting range of GCSEs and vocational qualifications. It could commence with a cross-curricular theme at age 14 – 'Stitching across the curriculum'. Level 1 would be 'stitch on a button', level 2 'stitch up a torn garment', level 3 'stitch up a patient', and level 4, for would-be right-wing politicians only, 'stitch up the Prime Minister'. Blobby Blobby Blobby.

28 January 1994

Minister squeezed by the ticklist tendency

As a lover of fiction I always enjoy reading what the right wing has to say about recent educational history. It beats Salvador Dali for imagination, Monty Python for humour and Torvill and Dean for artistic impression. I give it straight sixes for light relief. There I am wondering what has been happening in education, when up pops someone from the right wing with the latest side splitter.

Among recent rib-ticklers has been Michael Fallon blaming someone or other for reducing the National Curriculum to a 'box-ticking banality'. But remind me again, Mike, weren't you a member of the Government and a junior minister in education at the very time when all the box ticking was being pushed through, to howls of protest from the teaching profession?

He also lambasts comprehensive schools, because in one in three local authorities, the number of pupils obtaining five high grade (A to C) GCSEs is below a third, blaming the demise of the 11-plus for this. But is it not the case, Mike, that back in the days for which you and John Major yearn, below 20 per cent obtained such grades? By 1983 it was 27 per cent, and now, in the bad days of comprehensive schooling, it is nearer 40 per cent. Never spoil a decent prejudice with a bit of evidence, I always say.

More recently Sheila Lawlor of the Centre for Policy Studies, writing in the *Observer* about what is called the 'crazy' National Curriculum, says it was systematically imposed 'by the regiments of the education "service": teacher trainers, inspectors, education officials and theorists, exam boards and teachers'. Yet these are the very people who have opposed the craziness of its over-full prescription, and pleaded with Sir Ron Dearing to thin it out so that it is manageable.

It could be fun to re-write history by inverting a few things. 'Whoops, I appear to have stabbed myself,' said Julius Caesar. 'Don't commit suicide, you fool, we need you,' shrieked Brutus and Cassius. Why did King Harold thrust an arrow into his own eye? Why were the Europeans so unsporting as to throw things at Genghis Khan, just because he innocently turned up with a few thousand friends for a picnic outside their cities? Here, then, is my own potted history of the evolution of the National Curriculum. Only the facts have been changed.

'I think we need a national curriculum, Thatcher, so I'll go and consult the teaching profession,' said Kenneth Baker, 'but don't tell the press, we don't want the cameras round here.' The Prime Minister listened intently. 'You're so decisive, Kenneth,' she whispered. 'Of course you must see what people think, we don't want to upset anybody.'

Six months later they met again. 'We've got a bit of a problem, Thatcher,' said Kenneth Baker dismissively. 'The teachers don't want to teach. They much prefer ticking boxes instead. They've asked for everything to be required by law so that it occupies 150 per cent of the week, with lots and lots of silly tests. And they want it all written down in at least forty or fifty ring-bound folders.'

'Well, if that's what they want, then we must obey their wishes,' the Prime Minister acquiesced.

Three years later a similar meeting took place. 'I hope the teachers are all happy with the National Curriculum, because they do work so hard and I want them to have a whopping salary rise,' said the new Prime Minister to his Secretary of State. 'Well I've been up all night reading several books on curriculum theory,' said Kenneth Clarke, flicking a speck of dust off his immaculately pressed Chester Barrie suit, 'and I'm wondering if it's too strongly influenced by Erasmus and the rational humanists, and too little by empiricists such as Comenius.'

'I'd like a touch more empiricism,' said the Prime Minister, 'I re-read Comenius's *Orbis Sensualium Pictus* in the original only last night, as well as a couple of books by Professors Hirst and Peters. See if you can squeeze out a few of the spelling tests to make more time for reflection.'

'I would,' replied Clarke, 'but it's those bloody teachers. They just want more and more folders, lots of changes every few weeks and bags of silly tests.'

It is now 1993. 'We've got a bit of a problem with the education service again,' said John Patten. 'As you know, I've been attending all the conferences I can to chat to teachers, heads, parents and so on, and the teachers want to boycott this year's tests.'

'You are an old softy, you know, going round listening to everybody's point of view,' said the Prime Minister.

John Pattern cast his gaze away modestly. 'Well the teacher unions don't think their members have enough to do, so they want the National Curriculum and tests to be made more complex. Apparently, unless we increase the amount of testing, they're just going to boycott the whole thing.'

The Prime Minister looked perplexed. Having just agreed a 20 per cent pay increase for teachers, he was keen to see the further professionalization of teaching with longer training courses, more secondments, that sort of thing. Why oh why did teachers insist on such a complex curriculum? Why did they like ticking boxes rather than teaching? Why did they demand more and more national tests? Did they not have enough ring-bound folders already, and why did they insist on the curriculum being changed every few weeks?

'This is the biggest crisis we've ever faced in education, and only you can solve it,' he said to John Patten who blushed in that self-effacing way of his.

'There's only one possible solution then,' said Patten.

'You mean, call in Sir Ron Dearing?' said Major, lost in admiration at his minister's decisive brilliance.

'No,' replied Patten, 'get Michael Fallon and Sheila Lawlor to write in the newspapers about it.'

11 March 1994

No, nay, jamais, no more, Herr Hookhead

There is a game children play with each other. One child, usually an older one, will tell the others a story, purporting to be fact, usually with the sole aim of impressing the rest or scaring them witless. When I was a young primary school pupil, this streetwise older lad used to tell us stories about his dad giving him £5 a week spending money and how his uncle had a hook instead of a hand.

As we huddled together in a corner of the school yard listening to these fanciful tales as if they were genuine, it never occurred to us that, since the average wage at the time was £10 a week and his dad had an ordinary job, why would he give one son half his income, and what about his two brothers? Furthermore, why did someone on a fiver a week shoplift tomatoes from the greengrocer? Nor had anyone ever seen the uncle with the hook, but then part of the fairy tale was that he had emigrated to America. Gullible souls that we were, we believed every blood-curdling whopper.

Ever since then I have been a bit suspicious of snake oil salesmen who mention America. This perfectly rational prejudice was confirmed when the late great Kenneth Baker, El Supremo of the snake oil vendors, returned from one of his day trips to Disneyland or wherever he used to go, rabbiting on about city technology colleges, but saying nothing about the fact that the United States does not have a national curriculum.

The point about America is that you can find virtually anything there. You want to see some engaging nut teaching physics by swinging from a chandelier? Go to America. A school with its own Olympic-size swimming pool and multi-thousand-seater stadium, or one with 1,200 absentees a day, armed police in the classroom, and gun battles on the doorstep? Cross the Atlantic. Absolutely brilliant or utterly lousy teaching? Travel the USA. It is one of the most exciting places in the world, but you can bring back any traveller's tale you choose.

I try to visit every five years or so, and I recently went to the American Educational Research Association conference, in itself a remarkable experience. Some 10,000 people attend, ranging from those who resemble earnest train spotters or delegates at the annual meat cleavers' convention to the odd snake oil salesman who makes Kenneth Baker look like a wilting violet. In general, however, it is a marvellous opportunity to hear about some of the very best educational research.

One fascinating event is the ritual exchange between the British contingent and the rest of the world. 'Is it true that your seven-year-olds have to study the Aztecs by law?' some bewildered delegate from the Land of the Free will ask. 'Yes yes,' reply the Brits, launching into an impromptu cabaret act about the tons of paper, the ring-bound folders and the minister with a hook instead of a head. 'But didn't your teachers protest?' 'Yes yes,' we all say, warming to it, 'lots of letters were written to Hookhead and ultimately the Department for Education incinerator.' 'But didn't the politicians listen?' 'No no. Definitely no listening.' 'So why didn't your teachers riot?' Brits retire to the bar, brains hooked beyond repair.

Similar international exchanges take place in sign language, franglais, Bakerspeak . . . 'Non non, nous ne riotons pas en Angleterre' . . . 'Et ce Monsieur Hookhead, il n'écoute jamais?' . . . 'Ja ja, wir haben viele viele Attainment Targets, Profile Components und Programmes von Study, aber die Engländer rioten nicht' . . . 'Wer ist dieser Herr Hakenkopf?' Hundreds of dazed researchers return to their sundry homes, sadly shaking their heads at the mysteries of British tolerance and gallows humour.

What is even better than baffling foreigners is dispelling a few of the myths that get put our way by politicians, eager to impose their policies by telling everyone how well their particular prejudice works in America. On one occasion this happened in reverse and the American free market fan who tried to tell the audience how trouble-free imposing a market had been in Britain was nearly lynched by a normally mild-mannered member of the British party.

I was particularly interested in hearing about performance-related pay, which we are often told is in widespread use in the United States.

One researcher analysed what has happened in the past 10 years in 50 states, following a statement from a US governor in 1984 that 'not one state has paid one teacher one penny more for teaching well'.

Initially state governors vied with each other to boast that their state would be the first to introduce a fully fledged performance-related pay scheme. In reality 21 out of the 50 states never even started a scheme – so then there were 29. Of these 29, six introduced legislation or regulations, but abandoned the idea – so then there were 23.

Of these 23 states, 14 made a start in the mid-1980s, but soon withdrew – so then there were nine. Of these nine states, two are finding a decrease in the use of the schemes, and two others are likely to fold – so then there were five. Even in the five states that appear to have viable programmes, there is concern about the high costs of implementation, hostility from teachers and lack of co-operation from the unions.

So there you have it. Snake oil salesmen everywhere can make of it what they will. Tennessee and Texas are still keen, so quote them if you like the idea. Some 45 states either never bothered, or soon packed it in, so use that as evidence if you wish. There is no doubt about two things if elaborate performance-related pay schemes are introduced universally here: les Anglais ne rioteront pas, and Herr Hookhead or his successor won't read teachers' letters, or listen either.

22 April 1994

Mountains of mail urn their rightful place

As I opened my morning mail the other day, I suddenly thought of a great scheme for saving the Post Office a lot of money. All they have to do is steam open any letters addressed to educational establishments, send them to all the hospitals in the land, and, if laughter is the greatest cure, thousands of people will leap out of their sick beds, take to the streets and share their mirth with passers-by. The National Health Service will surely pay the Post Office millions for such a service every day.

Take the various missives that arrived on my desk one morning recently. The first was from Whizzo Toilet Rolls Inc., or some such, extolling the virtues of their toilet rolls for schools service.

'We provide schools with the cheapest toilet rolls and tissues available anywhere in the United Kingdom,' the accompanying blurb trilled breathlessly.

Now steady on Whizzo, or you might find the advertising standards people round your neck. The Department for Education has been providing schools for years with unlimited supplies of not just cheap, but absolutely free toilet paper. There were a few complaints about the, in the circumstances, aptly named White Paper 'Choice and Diversity' being a bit user unfriendly to anyone with haemorrhoids, and several requests from heads for the Parent's Charter to be published in ready perforated form, but on the whole the DFE has been peerless and tireless in its supply of alternative bog rolls.

Then there was a letter from a teacher wondering where all the people from the Office for Standards in Education would sit in her school, since it had cramped classrooms. The front-line Ofstedder can sit on a chair in the back corner, pen and hymn sheet poised, fair enough. But if that takes up any available spare space, where does the real HMI sit who is checking out that the new style Ofstedder is Ofstedding properly? And what about the mysterious third party, thought to be a would-be apprentice Ofstedder, who is shadowing the Ofstedder's Ofstedder?

Should this impressive phalanx sit behind each other in a rising line, like the multiple judges at the end of a hand-timed sprint race? Might a special gantry be strung from the ceiling to accommodate the whole lot, or should they stand on each other's shoulders, like a circus act, tottering round the room as they tick their checklists and performance indicator clipboards? What is the correct collective noun in the circumstances? An overdose of Ofstedders?

My next piece of mail was a cutting about Sheffield, my home town. Apparently the local crematorium was thrown open to the public and 600 people turned up 'for a day out'. What could this mean? I know that the citizens of my birthplace have a taste for the surreal, and tend to pursue low cost pleasures, but there must have been a simpler explanation.

It was probably 600 teachers looking for somewhere to incinerate all their pre-Dearing National Curriculum documents. It might even have been a cheap side trip organized as a bit of respite for a conference of Ofstedders. Perhaps the hotels are getting too expensive and Ofsted was trying out a pilot scheme in Sheffield.

In future Ofstedders will be trained in the local crematorium. Up to now, in areas where they are desperate for lay inspectors, they have only been recruited there. Still, that could resolve the classroom accommodation problem. Even tiny schools can surely find space for three small urns.

The most worrying missive, however, was a letter from someone claiming to have it on good authority that Patten would get the bullet in June and speculating about his successor. However, before the bonfires are lit, the street parties organized, the Spam sandwiches brought out and vintage bottles of early 40s Tizer cracked open, remember that one hopefully wild guess has been that Iain Sproat might succeed him. Some of his parliamentary colleagues are supposed to have liked his speech suggesting that teachers should spend 10 hours a week taking games after school for one and six pence farthing an hour, or whatever the going rate was in the good old days. I noticed that Iain Sproat's name is an anagram of 'I no is a prat', a trifle askew grammatically, but very reassuring.

A more chilling suggestion for Patten's successor is the name of John Redwood. In the best Baker-Clarke-Patten tradition, he recently wrote a newspaper article in *The Times* in which he attacked education, on this occasion universities. All the good ideas came from across the Atlantic, from think tanks and from city analysts, he claimed, presumably referring to the dotty rantings of the raving right wing. He wondered where the experts were that the nation needed to solve its problems. Trying to get his government to listen to them would be one answer. On and on he raged, about the excess of classifying and counting, 'expunging all spark of individual dignity'. At least he has been looking at the SATs and league tables.

I have a simple solution to Patten's impending departure. The ideas from the loony right-wing think tanks should all be incinerated in the local crematorium. They should be put into what would only need to be a very small urn. This casket of ashes would immediately be made Secretary of State and be put on display in the DFE entrance hall.

Several benefits would accrue. Patten's present room, said to consist of a throne and four mirrors, would be released for other purposes. It would also be an environmentally sound and space-saving solution.

The little casket would rapidly become the most successful member of
the Cabinet. But the greatest bonus would be that it would create far
less mayhem than the present incumbent, so it would certainly urn
my respect.

6 May 1994

Your right to be duped in your own home

Dear householder,

The Government has pleasure in sending you your copy of the
Parent's Charter. This costs even more than the one we sent to you in
1991, and is an amendment of the patronizing version leaked to the
press a few months ago.

If you are a parent you should read it carefully (oops, a bit of
patronizing slipped in there). If you are a 93-year-old pensioner you
may well wonder why we have wasted a seven-figure sum sending this
to you and millions like you. Well, what with VAT on fuel and that
sort of thing, you can always club together with a few other geriatrics
next winter and burn the things to keep warm. That should save you
a few quid to spend on bingo, or whatever you peasants do with your
welfare cash nowadays.

Lots of rights
The major reason for sending you this charter is to hoodwink you
into thinking that you have lots of rights. You should know that you
have the right to have lots of rights; send your child to a school with
a leaking roof; run car-boot sales if your school is skint; and have your
children taught by teachers who are overworked, underpaid and
usually completely knackered by Wednesday afternoon. So you see,
you have bags and bags of rights, honest.

Types of school
There are lots of schools for you to choose from, so many we can
hardly remember them all. You can choose one of the following:

Private schools: these are really good – small classes, interesting things to smoke, all the toffs send their children there. It will cost you a bob or two, so fork out, meanie!

City technology colleges: we like these best, so we spend zillions of pounds on them. The children have about six microcomputers each. They even stack microcomputers in piles in the school yard to make goal posts for a lunch-time kick-about. It's a gas!

Grant-maintained schools: you'd better get used to these, because they're all you'll have in future if we get our way. As a parent, you have a free vote, so long as you vote 'Yes' (just kidding!).

LEA primary and secondary schools. The riff-raff have to go somewhere. If all else fails, send your child to one of these, but don't blame us if they catch lice.

Choosing a school

When the time comes to choose a school, you need to know that if you live in a rural area, tough toenails, there is no choice, so move to a town. If you are poor, then it serves you right for not being able to afford a chauffeur so your child can go outside the area. If the governors want their school to be top of the league, then forget it if your child is thick or a bit naughty. You should look at the local performance tables, which are available at any estate agents; these look very impressive, but they tell you nothing about education. You will find out where the rich kids live, however, so move house, sucker!

Testing and examinations

Pupils are tested at age 7, 11 and 14. The tests are designed to be 'easier to manage than in the past' (it says here on a piece of paper brought in by a man with a very big club in his hand). They assess children against national standards ('national' means 'compared with scores obtained by pupils in the three schools that did not actually boycott the tests').

Discipline

All schools must have discipline policies. These lay down rules such as no bonking (unless you're a Cabinet minister); no smoking (unless the tobacco company concerned makes contributions to party funding); no drinking (same as above); no money for books and equipment (might as well make it a school rule, since it happens anyway).

Even more rights

If you have been daft enough to swallow all the glossy tosh so far, then here are a few more rights you've got: the right to watch Office for Standards in Education inspections frighten the crap out of the head and staff; to have a whip round for the increasing number of teachers quitting the profession early; to foot the bill for the 90-fold increase in glossy government public relations bilge such as this charter; to vote Conservative; and to have a complete prat as a minister.

For further information send a cheque for as much as you can afford, made out to The Please Please Re-elect Us Campaign, to the following address: 'There's More Where This Came From, Pinch of Salt, Connjob, Costa Billion'.

1 July 1994

Rank guide to the most ludicrous leagues

One of the few consolations to people suffering in education at the moment is that other professions are on the receiving end of the same sort of tripe. The explosive reaction of the medical profession to hospital league tables seemed to attract more publicity than was given to teachers' views of school league tables. The Government's reply to all this is to accuse professionals of wanting to hide the true state of affairs from their clients, thereby neatly avoiding any debate about what kind of 'truth' is represented in league tables.

Their latest wheeze is to talk of judging doctors and hospitals according to how many patients snuff it. This is, of course, tremendous news to staff employed in the ingrowing toenail ward, but has not been so well received by those working with the terminally ill. In these days of Whitehall farce, it had to come eventually – death, the ultimate performance indicator. As with school league tables, the starting point is being ignored. I keep hoping that, if Linford Christie gives me a 99-metre start, the Government will acclaim me as the fastest man on Earth for crossing the finishing line of the 100-metre race ahead of him.

With luck league tables will spread everywhere and their credibility simply implode, as quality is ignored and quantity revered. Who will be top vicar in the Soul-Saving league, and will clerics at the bottom be put in Purgatory? I shall move ahead of Rembrandt and Rubens in the Biggest Paintings league, by tipping buckets of paint randomly over even bigger canvases than theirs. In the Acme Garden Shed Writer of Most Novels league, Barbara Cartland will top Dickens and Tolstoy. Orchestras will pay bass drummers a higher performance-related salary than violinists, for making more noise. Conductors, who produce no more than the occasional swish, will be paid nothing.

It is the Eurovision Song Contest view of human performance. Millions of people give rapt attention to 20 absolutely appallingly naff and completely forgettable dirges, the Albanian 'Sh-boom, sh-boom' indistinguishable from the Ruritanian 'La la la, hi ho hum'. Yet they all seem fascinated by the brain-corroding climax, an hour of vote-counting that produces the final league table of winners and losers, but does absolutely nothing for the quality of music in the world.

Perhaps the Government should import the Eurovision and World Cup paraphernalia into education, leagues and all. Next year aspects of education could be shown throughout the Continent, with judging panels led by smiling chairmen who speak neither English, nor, so far as one can tell, their native language, announcing the votes of 20 national juries – 'For the British entry, "Remember Me?" by Johnny Patten and the Has-beens *nul points.*'

Like over-lenient World Cup referees, teachers who fail to put pupil offenders into detention could be sent home. Heads could pick two substitutes for teachers suffering from exhaustion, though no doubt Department for Education officials would be standing at the classroom door insisting that no one could come in or out until the relevant form had been filled in. Yellow and red cards could be waved at ministers for tackling the education system from behind, or kicking teachers in the groin.

The next Parent's Charter will probably look like the back of the *Sports Echo* on a Saturday night, spangled with oodles of leagues, as the 'right to know' argument is wheeled out as an excuse for even bigger glossy brochures. My mother rang me up a couple of weeks ago. She had just got her copy of the Parent's Charter – was there anything she should be doing? I told her it was her 83rd birthday present from the Government and put her mind at rest by pointing out that I was through the education system now, so her responsibilities had ceased.

All this narrow, myopic policy is part of the same discredited market model, collapsing under the weight of its stupidity, but still persisted with by the Government. Another manifestation of it is the current attitude to adult education. To qualify for Government support nowadays, courses for adults have to demonstrate that they will improve national productivity and prosperity. There is nothing wrong with the nation trying to be more productive or prosperous – what is mistaken is the attempt to restrict financial support to certain courses.

Is becoming cultured a contribution to national prosperity? Suppose education, sport, youth work, all help reduce yobbery, then in order to win financial support, does an explicit link to the production of more spigots or ball bearings have to be established? Will music tuition only be offered to people who can argue that they will one day become a pop millionaire like Paul McCartney and sell millions of records abroad? Is education no longer a right?

Thousands of retired people who have attended university extra-mural classes for years on archaeology, philosophy or life sciences, are being told they must sign up for certificates, write essays and be examined, so that it can be argued they are acquiring qualifications to 'improve national productivity'. The present generation of school-children may have 30 or 40 years of healthy retirement. It is ludicrous to tie their adult education to a spurious notion of 'productivity', so they can be rank-ordered in some meaningless geriatrics' league table.

I look forward to more and more league tables next session – Britain's worst bishops, best undertakers, heaviest deputy heads, craziest lay inspectors, sexiest school governors, most knackered standard assessment task markers. Hottest competition of all will no doubt come at the top of the Daftest Minister league. Have a good summer.

15 July 1994

He came with little baggage, left with the sack

'He is the worst, isn't he?' During the past two years teachers and heads, well used to being under the cosh from a succession of politicians, frequently reached the sad conclusion that John Patten was walking off with the ministerial booby prize. From people who had become adept, where ministers were concerned, at making fine discriminations at the wooden-spoon end of the spectrum, it was a damning indictment.

Yet it should have been very different. In April 1992, after Kenneth Baker's unctuous tenure and the uncouth indifference of Kenneth Clarke, Patten only had to stay on his feet to score with a profession that desperately needed a break from deprecation. He came to the job with little baggage, other than, like Baker and Clarke before him, the faint hint that he was a 'liberal', and that is where his problems started. Baker and Clarke had already demonstrated what ambitious ministers with liberal pedigrees would do to please the dominant right-wing of their party. Those tagged 'liberal' have to spend all their time showing what macho guys they are, so they talk foolishly tough.

From the beginning John Patten came over as deeply insecure, hence what seemed to be his permanent search for a mirror in which to preen himself. For the first few months he was known as 'the invisible man'. Sightings were rare, as he turned down invitations to conferences routinely accepted by previous ministers. It was as if he were afraid to venture out and give his new right-wing image a public airing. One wondered whether he sat at home rehearsing his lines: 'I'm mean. I'm tough. I don't give a hang . . . No, wait a minute, how about: Listen to me scumbags. Eat dirt. I, er . . . You're all Luddites . . . yes, that's it, you hear me? So there (stamps foot).'

It simply did not work. When he did eventually appear in public he went to the other extreme, racing from the radio car to the television studio, the conference hall and back again. Unfortunately he picked up a yellow card almost every time he tried to join the game. Some were for silly trivial offences, the equivalent of asking the referee if he had forgotten his glasses. Others were more significant, such as his comments about parents' national representatives holding Neanderthal views, when concern for parents was supposed to lie at the very heart of the Government's policies.

Page one of any ministerial handbook on how to manage 25,000 schools and 430,000 teachers should say: 'Try to give the impression at least that you are on the same side as other people, even if you have to criticise them from time to time.' Perhaps John Patten did despise teachers, but I suspect it was another example of his own insecurity coming out as contempt. He got further yellow cards when he left the Newcastle conference of the National Association of Headteachers, saying he was too busy to stay and answer questions, but then stood outside the conference hall after his session talking to journalists, in full view of all the heads he had just abandoned.

Even on *Blue Peter* he could not get it right with his audience, in this case a group of well-behaved children. He was like Captain Troy of the *Thunderbirds*, strings pulled by some invisible manipulator from the Right. A worried boy asked about the test-score league table: 'Most of the children in our school are Asian, and English is our second language. It makes our school look bad.' 'Beep beep', went Troy. 'Take evasive action', seemed to be the instruction from the captain of the starfleet.

'You and I are both English, aren't we?' he began, strings twitching merrily. *Thunderbirds* were go. Flannel, flannel . . .. 'English is the most popular language in the whole of the world . . . it's therefore very important indeed that everyone who goes to school in England, from wherever they come from.' From wherever they come from? This surely, was a giveaway that whoever had programmed him before the show had put at least one instruction in upside down.

More yellow cards piled up – the Mum's Army of unqualified parents who were apparently good enough to teach infants with little or no training; the ill-conceived attempt to detach teacher training from universities and bury schools under more demands, contrary to the trend in other countries which are strengthening the higher-education component; the naked bribes offering highly funded technology programmes only to schools that opted out; the Tim Brighouse affair; the repeated testing boycotts.

Many of these problems arose directly from John Major's office, and Major survives while Patten perishes. But then, that is all part of the same problem, as Major, too, must keep peace with the ranting right wing. It seemed sad that in Patten's last days he was said to be offering yet more ideas to Major, when the education system desperately needed less ideology and more pragmatism.

In November 1992 I wrote in *The Times Educational Supplement* that, for bowing the knee uncritically to the right wing, John Patten would eventually disappear into oblivion, like Egon Krenz, the East German leader. Perhaps it was another indication of his insecurity that he tried to ban *The TES* from the Department for Education as a result.

In the end, the yellow cards simply became too many and too frequent to ignore. He had to leave the pitch. Many of his parliamentary colleagues and a large number of Conservative local politicians cannot now find a good word for him. I suspect he will not be picked for the first team again.

29 July 1994

5

The men from the ministry

Throughout the fifteen years or so covered in this collection of articles those working in education became more and more conscious of the 'Ministry', first the Department of Education and Science, then, after 1992, the Department for Education. The first few articles in this chapter come from the early years of the 1980s, when the DES merely flexed its muscles. By the second half of the chapter and the 1990s, everything has gone mad, with quangos all over the place, a view of management that suggested teachers were androids and children were commodities, and a form of school inspection by the Office for Standards in Education that was pure George Orwell.

Secret service

'Hello, is that the DES?' Can you put me through to information please?'

'Open or classified?'

'I'm sorry, I don't understand.'

'Do you want open information or the secret stuff?'

'Well, I want to know when the survey of first schools is going to be published so that we can put on an in-service course for teachers.'

'That sounds as if it could be a bit hush hush, I'll put you through to the mole.'

'Hello, Deep Throat here.'

'Look, I don't quite follow what's going on. I just wanted to ask when the HMI report on first schools was due, and I was put through to you, something about *classified information*, and *a mole?*'

'Quite correct, I'm master in charge of leaks, so to speak. You see, some of the lads got so fed up with politicians deliberately leaking confidential information to further their sordid little ambitions, we decided to set up our own "reliable sources close to the government" agency. I mean, it's fair enough, damn it. Five minutes after a cabinet meeting and anyone will tell you the colour of Miss Piggy's garters for a couple of gin and tonics, but if one of us whispers a word there's a public inquiry and some poor sod gets his vitals severed?'

'But how does it work?'

'Easy. There are three categories: "hot", "extra hot" and "pass the asbestos gloves, Ethel". Which would you like?'

'Well, I only wanted to know about the survey . . .'

'Tell you what, try a "hot" one for starters. Did you know that on the day Baroness Whatsit left, Rhodes Boyson was there with his pantechnicon at the crack of dawn to bag her large office before the new boys got there first. Scout's honour. I tripped over his tea-chests in the lift myself.'

'I suppose you'll be getting used to the new ministers for a bit.'

'We're not over the moon, I can tell you. I mean Mark Carlisle really *listened*. He didn't understand a blind word, mind you, but he listened with that likeable glazed look of his. We'd heard a couple of Tory intellectuals might be shipped in, but usually that only means three or four CSEs. Instead two bloody Fellows of All Souls. I'm all for having one of two toffs, we could do with a bit of class after some of the Labour scruff we've had to put up with, but Sir Monty Python as chief bottle-washer was a bit of a shock.'

'Has he made an impact yet?'

'That's what bothers us. After his 1974 Birmingham speech about more birth control for the lower orders, we're a bit worried he might be buying a few crates of contraceptives with Union Jacks stamped on them for HMIs to dole out to the proletariat on their rounds. So far he's only sent us a short memo asking (a) how much of Conservative manifesto policy has been implemented? (b) what are HMI doing about improving discipline in schools? I wrote back (a) fortunately very little, (b) caning the little buggers, and signed it "Wedgwood Benn". Well, you have to laugh so you don't cry.'

'Won't you get into trouble?'

'Who me? No, I'm demob happy, retire in a couple of weeks, that's why I'm in charge of leaks. How about this one for a scorcher? You know that a senior civil servant was asked to do a report on the inspectorate, well he goes through the service with a fine tooth comb and the HMI come out smelling sweeter than violets. Need to fire one or two who died on the job and stayed on posthumously, but apart from that the best thing since fish fingers. So what happens? Sir Derek Thingy, you know the Marks and Spencer's man put in to bash the bureaucrats – and you tell me what a fellow who's a wizard on Y-fronts and seamless tights can possibly know about education – anyway he sends it back and says it's all wrong. Now angry letters are flying back and forth and we just hide under the table. Do you want photocopies, by the way?'

'Well I really only wanted to know about . . .'

'Did you know the voucher scheme is being resurrected?'

'You mean the one Rhodes Boyson turned down?'

'Bullseye. Collect a few vouchers and a couple of Persil packet flaps and the poor suckers think they can all send their kids to Eton. Well we've been told to get that out again. Then there's Manchester's tertiary college scheme, that's the biggie. We'd just got Carlisle on the point of signing that one by telling him it was his travel voucher to the PAT conference when, bingo, he gets the elbow and the new boys decide to make a big issue out of it.'

'It could have been worse, you might have got Heseltine.'

'We might have got Ken Dodd, at least there would have been a few laughs. What was it, by the way, that you were asking me about?'

'The publication date of the HMI survey of first schools.'

'Ah yes. Sorry squire, can't tell you that, it's confidential.'

2 October 1981

Sounds familiar

'Good morning, Minister. It's very kind of you to agree to meet us in the middle of what must be a very busy schedule, but as university vice-chancellors we felt we must put you in the picture about what is happening to higher education.'

'There can be no going back on our policy of substantial reductions in public expenditure.'

'Yes indeed, Minister, I appreciate your difficulties. Perhaps I can introduce my two colleagues. Dr Peter Jackson is vice-chancellor of Burnley University, Professor John Hardcastle is Principal of the School of Really Careful Dentistry at Barnstaple University, and I am Sir Jeremy Fitzwarren, Head of Grimsby University and currently Chairman of the Federation of Vice Chancellors.'

'There can be no going back on our policy of substantial reductions in public expenditure.'

'We understand your dilemma, Minister, and indeed the universities have already taken their share of cuts just like any other sector, but at Burnley University we face the loss of £4 million in two years, and we are by no means untypical. Every university is in the same boat. In simple terms: if we don't sack people we go bankrupt, and if we do sack them we go bankrupt because of all the redundancy payments.'

'There can be no going back on our policy of substantial reductions in public expenditure.'

'Minister, let me translate this into human terms. More than 20,000 places will be lost. Well-qualified youngsters who have worked hard at school will not get a university education. There will be thousands of redundancies among university staff of all kinds, lecturers, technicians, cleaners, porters, secretaries. Some of our best courses will simply have to be closed down. Now we beg you to reconsider, perhaps give us five years for the run-down instead of two.'

'There can be no going back on our policy of substantial reductions in public expenditure.'

'May we put it to you in economic terms, Minister? It costs the country £4,380 per unemployed person according to MSC figures, so it is actually cheaper to send people to university. The price of all redundancies could be of the order of 300 or 400 million pounds. It would cost less to keep the people in their jobs than fire them. Can't you see that the rundown of universities makes no economic sense either?'

'There can be no going back on our policy of substantial reductions in public expenditure.'

'Hardcastle, Jackson, come over hear a minute. Look, have you noticed how the Minister gives us the same reply no matter what we've said, and how his face never changes expression and he never blinks. That old story in *The Sunday Times* must have been true.'

'What story in *The Sunday Times*?'

'You remember, back in the sixties, how the Russians or the Chinese or someone had developed a top secret new artificial human technology, and had planted a couple of androids high up in every Western European administration, specially programmed to wreck the economy. It was thought to be quite ridiculous at the time, but it might be true. What do you think? Him and Norman Tebbit?'

'Perhaps you'd better test it out Fitzwarren, it seems utterly fantastic to me.'

'Right then. Er, we've been thinking, Minister. One way to solve our problems would be if we were all to link arms and sing a couple of verses of Eskimo Nell.'

'There can be no going back on our policy of substantial reductions in public expenditure.'

'Oh my God Jackson, it's true. No wait, one more test to be absolutely   certain. Er, Minister. What about this for a possible solution? Ying tong, ying tong, ying tong, flip flop, oodle noodle.'

'There can be no going back on our policy of substantial reductions in public expenditure.'

'Look this is absolutely dreadful, we must do something quickly. Hardcastle, you get on to Fleet Street and sell the story to the highest bidder, that should cover a few redundancy payments. Jackson, you guard the door. I'd better get on to the Prime Minister. Damn it, where's the Downing Street number? Here it is on this pad. Come on, answer the phone, will you. Ah, Prime Minister, thank goodness, at last. Look, no time to explain, but this is a national emergency. I'm Sir Jeremy Fitzwarren, and we've just been talking to the Minister about universities, and I think you ought to know . . .'

'There can be no going back on our policy of substantial reductions in public expenditure.'

27 November 1981

Here comes yet another bundle of joy

I used to love getting parcels. There was a time when, if the postman actually rang the bell, you knew there was a parcel for you. It may well be a pullover from Auntie Edna, two sizes too big in lurid yellow, but never mind, a parcel was a parcel, and so far as I was concerned it was Santa time. If you had to sign for it, all the better, as it was probably valuable.

Nowadays my heart sinks when the postman comes towards me brandishing a pencil. Even worse when he is someone dressed in a purple cap with a name like 'Quiktrip' on it. You know it is a government agency using some dyslexic privatized delivery company that took twice as long and cost three times as much as the Post Office. No wonder the Government rabbits on about 'delivering' the curriculum.

The parcel usually contains printed matter and you probably have to sign for it so you cannot pretend you never received it. The faint whirring sound in the distance is a new-style, privatized HMI hiding in the bushes making a video of the handover. Paranoia is alive and well in these mad times.

I suppose if you are a grant-maintained school then it is likely that some of your parcels are offers of trillions of pounds for things that ordinary schools are denied, like bundles of readies to become a technology college. I wonder if these are delivered by the man from 'Kikback', the Government's seedy bribe laundering agency.

Perhaps you have to go to a remote telephone box or transport cafe car park and know the right password ('We've opted out') before receiving your package, or 'Cashpak' as it is known in Government circles. You then sign with a pseudonym like Al Capone or Bugsy Malone.

Anyway, my latest missive came from the Office for Standards in Education. It was the enormous 500-page (well, 493 pages actually) Handbook for the Inspection of Schools, in a huge ring-bound folder that makes National Curriculum documents look positively puny.

Many words can be used to describe it. Certainly it is thorough. The problem is, however, that is so ludicrously over the top, so massively over-complex and bureaucratic, it will defeat the simple purpose for which it was designed.

Far from improving schools, it merely creates a sense of being beleaguered, a dangerous Dunkirk spirit, inimical to the positive atmosphere needed for genuine improvement.

It will put the frighteners on every school in the land and is a certain cure for any heads who are constipated. It takes a sledge-hammer to crush your nuts. I wish someone would apply the same searing scrutiny to the Government's seedy and unfair education policies. If you have not seen it, here are a few extracts.

Team composition: one registered inspector, one butcher, one estate agent (to write the report), five people from the bus station.

How to refer to people: Teachers ('you lot'), head ('scumbag'), business people ('sir').

Rating scales: A five-point rating scale will be used: 1 = excellent, have you thought of moving to a grant-maintained school? 2 = good, what are you doing in the maintained sector? 3 = satisfactory, how come you're still sane with all this tripe going on? 4 = poor, have you thought of becoming a minister? 5 = hello, Mr Patten.

Performance indicators: A wide range of performance indicators will be used: (1) test scores (2) scores on tests (3) how children got on when they were tested.

Pre-inspection Context and School Indicator (PICSI) reports: before an inspection registered inspectors will be supplied with a PICSI report, a HOBGLOBIN report (any weird characters on the staff) and a WHOOPSI report (the inside story of the head's affair with the senior mistress).

Observing lessons: inspectors who know what they are doing should use the lesson observation pro forma provided. Lay inspectors should tick one of the following statements: (1) 'Would have benefited from National Service' (2) 'Teachers, guv, I'd string 'em all up' (3) 'Gosh, they don't sit in rows any more'.

Statutory requirements: any breaches of the law must be reported. You should be able to get them on assemblies, but if that fails try 'Did you boycott the tests then? or 'All right, smartass, but are you teaching the Aztecs?'

Failing schools: Where it is decided a school is failing a suitable form of words should be used with the head, expressed subtly, like: 'This school is the crappiest outfit we have ever set eyes on'. The written report must use the following approved wording 'This school has low test scores, is in an inner-city area and the parents probably vote Labour, so Ministers don't like it and it is officially deemed to be failing. We shall, therefore, send in two terminally bewildered retired colonels who will make bog all difference, but it will look good.'

Guidance on writing the report: essential features to include are (1) an analysis of test scores; (2) examination results; (3) a clearly worded statement saying 'Can I have the money now please?'

Relations with OFSTED: registered inspectors have a contract with OFSTED. Any who go round the twist during an inspection will receive a contract from another Government agency OFFTHEWALL and immediately be put on a quango. Those who disagree with what they are asked to do will receive a contract from a third agency, which deals with schools, called SODOFF.

Post-inspection: When the inspection is over there are four absolutely crucial matters that must be completed: (1) order the school to opt out no matter what kind of report it gets; (2) indicate the availability, at a suitable price, of the Government's privatized advisory service 'Quikfix'; (3) take the money; (4) and run.

8 October 1993

Sleeping the sleep of the just about with it

It never ceases to amaze me how willing many lay people are to become involved in education. Perhaps it is not too surprising that parents show interest and give time, because their own children are involved, but thousands of public-spirited souls still volunteer to be school governors, despite the back-breaking load.

The time when governors met in the school library once a year, for a cake, a sausage roll, a cup of tea, largely to decide the date and time of the next meeting, is long since gone.

In any case the sausage roll, if it still exists, is probably a National Curriculum technology assignment, so they have to grade it on the ten-level scale; the cake and cup of tea are provided by the recently privatized Swineshire Business Unit Vomitarium plc; most of the governors have to employ Securicor to bring along the half-hundredweight of papers they have been sent; and the school library charges them a £50 room hire fee.

I was a little surprised, therefore, to read of a senior police officer, talking about crime in Britain, describing how master criminals are very well disguised today, blending neatly and imperceptibly into the local landscape. There are about 400 big-time crime bosses, he revealed, all brilliantly concealed in our towns and villages: 'Their children go to the right schools, they may even be school governors.'

'Shock, horror, scandal!', you exclaim. Yes, you thought Mrs Sanderson was the parent who chaired Swineshire Primary governors, but the awful truth is that by night she is known to Swineshire police as Dolly the drugs baroness. Mr Archibald, chairman of the appointments sub-committee? Not merely the owner of the local newsagents, but The Bald Cougar, fearless safe cracker.

Governors' meetings will never be the same again, as members look at each other speculatively across the table. Is sweet little Mrs Wimpole the Swineshire Arsonist? (And if so, could she please burn the school down so we can get a decent new building.) Does upright Mr Blandly-Smiling, the local estate agent, fence silverware in his spare time? Is the amicable vicar really ace card sharp Mick the Vic?

What about the head? He rolled up to the last governors' meeting in a brand new second-hand Vauxhall Viva. But did he buy it or nick it? And if the stock cupboard is a bit fuller recently, is it because the head and governors went out ram-raiding after their last meeting? I know times are hard financially in education and the Government wants schools to find extra resources, but if the source of the newly acquired loot was not minuted, questions must be asked.

We are lucky that so many public-spirited people give freely of their time and energy, but the contribution of lay participants in education should nonetheless be carefully scrutinized. If not, then the well-intentioned amateur can step over an increasingly faint dividing line between proper citizen's interest and professional expertise. I once met the chairman of one of the thousands of educational quangos in existence nowadays, who used to greet people with the words: 'I know nothing about education. By the way, please call me Humphrey.'

The message seemed to be that, so far as education was concerned, Christian-name mateyness was a fair swop for professional expertise. But would society accept this in the case of other professional groups? 'This is your pilot speaking. Welcome to Grotti Airline's flight to Benidorm. I know nothing about aviation. By the way, please call me Humphrey.' Never mind calling him Humphrey, how about calling the police?

The same unease persists about the role of lay inspector in OFSTED inspections. According to the 492-page *How to inspect a school* handbook, lay inspectors should do everything that the other inspectors do, even if the latter are seasoned professionals and the lay inspector is as nutty as a fruitcake. I have no objection to lay inspectors coming along to give the non-professional's point of view on certain school matters, but they should be kept well away from purely professional affairs.

Analysing lessons and assessing the quality of teaching and learning needs a degree of professional expertise which very few lay inspectors could have acquired. Making a judgement about matters like the extent to which the work is appropriate to the individual child or group, the German teacher's linguistic accuracy, the skill with which teachers explain key concepts in physical sciences or mathematics, the class management strategies being employed, the understanding of how children of different backgrounds and ages actually learn a particular topic in class, are all beyond the direct experience of most lay inspectors.

I do not know if it was the lay member, but the true story of the OFSTED inspector who nodded off in lessons during an inspection did cause some hilarity. It is difficult to know how to respond. If an OFSTED inspector lapses into slumber during your lesson, how should you react? Should you be offended that your magnificent teaching has sent the observer into deep repose? Or merely sympathize with someone who finds earning £200 a day a little fatiguing? Or speculate whether he is dreaming of the glories of the Boer War?

Perhaps the word OFSTED will now enter the English language as a synonym for sleep. 'Had a late night yesterday, so I'm just going to have a little OFSTED before my afternoon teaching,' teachers will cheerily announce. Perhaps the well-concealed arch-criminal Mr Big will accidentally reveal his identity as a night-time safe cracker in the next governors' meeting, by lapsing into OFSTED during matters arising. You can't do a proper job as a governor nowadays, I always say, unless you make sure you have had eight hours decent OFSTED before the meeting.

25 February 1994

A quango to cap the lot of them

It is said that many Germans are so active on holiday that they arrive back home, go to see the doctor and are immediately told to take a vacation. Some teachers have recommenced school in September in the same state of fatigue. This is despite the consolation that John Patten, in a neatly ironic parallel to what was his ultimate dream for local education authority schools, has been compulsorily opted out and become a fully grant-maintained backbench MP.

Stress in the teaching profession is now endemic, rather than an end-of-term phenomenon, as became clear from the shocking information released in August, just before the new school year started, on ill health among teachers. The figures, no doubt 'broken down by age and sex', in the traditional words of the social science report, show a marked increase in those who have retired early through poor health. There may be a few caught up by the passing years, but I doubt if sex has played a part in it nowadays. The introduction of the National Curriculum and assessment did far more for birth control among teachers than the whole of the pill and condom industry put together.

Despite superfical promises that politicians might lay down their weapons and stop attacking teachers, a significant source of stress in recent years, the ceasefire did not last long, as the direct or oblique put-downs continued. Junior minister Robin Squire kept up the tradition by implying that the 90 per cent of teachers who did not teach in grant-maintained schools had 'second-class' status. Nice one squire. That should go down well in the teachers' ward of the Kenneth Baker Rest Home for the Prematurely Knackered. If Gillian Shephard is serious about supporting teachers and maintained schools, then she should be thrashing Squire with a knotted boot lace at this very second.

Fortunately help was at hand. One medical source said that the solution was lots of physical activity, as this was good therapy. Ten lengths of the pool, a dozen swings at the punchbag, a game of tennis or squash, a few press-ups, and all would be well. Millions of pain-killing endorphins surge through the wearied body and soul. I like the sound of it so much I am tempted to set up my own therapy clinic.

We at Happyteach plc will be offering the very latest in treatment. The gym will be full of those rubber punchbag figures, with a

weighted hemispherical base, that spring upright again when you hit them. All the figures will be crafted to look like recent education ministers, complete with clown costume, illuminated red nose and rotating bow tie.

Half-an-hour smacking the crap out of Kenneth Baker, Clarkie or Patten will restore the most jaded spirits. Hence our company motto 'Sod the SAT, bop the Patt'.

There will be rigorous medical screening of all participants in the Happyteach therapy course. Latest scientific detection techniques will be used to see if teachers are carrying the two most debilitating strains of bacteria, mainly picked up from reading documents on assessment, known as Streptocockup A and Streptocockup B.

Diet is also an important part of the programme. Our extensive menus include many features with which experienced teachers will be familiar. The day begins with a dog's breakfast, followed by noodles, tripe, waffles and fruity fools. A variety of sundowners are available, including SATpack on the Rocks and our new cocktail, Squire's Forrit, which is shaken but not stirred.

The best therapy of all, however, is that we find each patient a job on an educational quango. As you will know billions of pounds are now spent on education entirely by unelected quangos. Unfortunately teachers suffer two serious handicaps so far as the Government is concerned: they know something about education and they lack the odd fifty grand to contribute to its next general election fund.

We at Happyteach have therefore set up our own supreme body, the Quango Quango, which will be in charge of all education quangos and be staffed entirely by teachers who have been feeling the strain lately.

Sir Hubert Filing-Cabinet has agreed to chair it. He is ideal for the job, since he is a retired industrialist who knows bugger all about education and has just become an Office for Standards in Education lay inspector. It takes two to quango, so the first two vital jobs are ready to be advertised.

Head of memos

£120,000 to £150,000 (pay award pending).

You will be responsible for 5,000 members of staff. Your main duties will be to ensure that the flow of memos between them is constant and unremitting (performance-related bonus available). You will have twelve secretaries and your own photocopier.

Head of paper clips
£100,000–£115,000 (pay award pending).
You will mainly be responsible for sending boxes of paper clips to the Head of Memos. Recent experience of attaching paper clips to documents might be advantageous. A further important duty is to adapt the expensive carpet we have bought from the National Curriculum Council, by working out how the hell to unpick the NCC logo and crochet it into our QQ logo instead.

The Quango Quango will, of course, be an equal opportunities employer. There will be no discrimination and the severely knackered will stand just as good a chance as the mildly knackered. We have high hopes that even the most extreme cases of knackerment will respond to the therapy of being paid a fortune for doing something that nobody really needs, instead of being paid peanuts for doing something that everybody needs.

You'll know when you've been quangoed.

16 September 1994

That's how it goes, every Body knows

New readers begin here:
Performance-related pay for the teaching profession has been an aspiration of a number of government education ministers (Billy Smart, Fred Chipperfield, Ivor Circus). Several possibilities have been considered, and last year a firm of consultants looked at 15 schools, of which three were grant-maintained, to see how a performance-related pay scheme could be introduced.

Now the School Teachers' Review Body, at the office of (get this) Manpower Economics, 22 Kingsway, London WC2B 6JY, has put out a consultative paper on the issue. Replies have to be in by October 10. I have often written responses to an individual, or an organization, but never to a Body. So here goes.

Now read on:
Dear Body (forgive the familiarity).

Thank you for your paperette on performance-related pay. As I passed it on to a colleague, I experienced the same sense of loss as when my chicken pox scabs fell off many years ago.

You see, Body, your paperette is all wrong from the moment it says: 'In our view it is essential that the scheme should be kept as simple as possible.' That is precisely the problem. In my view it is essential that the scheme should be kept in the nearest deep underground mausoleum, precisely because it is not such an easy matter as you, Body, would like to believe.

Consider one example, in which the 'simple' principle occurs. You say: 'We propose, on grounds of simplicity, that the scheme would apply to heads and deputies who are formally paid as such; it would not cover other teachers.'

It is not a 'simple' matter to detach heads and deputies from other teachers, though this is precisely what the Government seeks to achieve, by picking off senior people, offering them more pay, haranguing them about their responsibility to give national tests, and threatening them with hit squads.

You justify this by claiming that senior people should be paid more when the class management in the school is good. Just imagine a school in which several teachers are running their socks off in difficult circumstances and where there is a pre-retired head, mentally in Provence most days, who picks up the loot for their efforts. That should do wonders for team spirit.

I haven't read anything as daft as your section headed Essential Performance Indicators since the School Examinations and Assessment Council passed quietly away. Was it wise, Body, to snip up old SEAC documents, glue them randomly together and then pour four bottles of vodka into the photocopier?

Or did some other miracle of modern technology produce such flawless gems as 'examination and key stage test results are the best measure of academic performance' and 'pupils' absence rates reflect the general well-being, ethos and managerial effectiveness of a school', or that the head's financial wizardry should be judged entirely on whether the school kept within its budget.

There were some choice examples of language in your paperette, Body. I particularly enjoyed the idea of a 'three-year rolling average'. Now I mustn't scoff, I know, because you were trying to say that if a school's exam results dipped one year, then it would be unfair to rip a few fivers back out of the poor head's wallet, so full marks for trying to even out the cruel vagaries of fate.

What cracked me up about the notion of a 'three-year rolling average' was the memory of one head, now long retired, who was notorious for his huge consumption of alcohol during school time and who was pretty mediocre as a result. 'Rolling average' summed him up neatly.

Another hysterical phrase was the bit about how heads would actually qualify for a performance award. Apparently financial expertise would be 'one of the essential indicators for triggering the release of funds'. I think 'triggering the release of funds' is what we simple-minded peasants used to term 'getting the money', but I have given up trying to use Government education patois nowadays, preferring English. Unless I misunderstood, of course, and heads have to use a sawn-off shotgun to get their bonus.

At the end of all this, a deputy head in a small school could get £300. According to your paperette this might have involved endless governors' meetings, analysis of all your daft performance indicators, the filling in of lots of forms, a possible 'detailed scrutiny by the Audit Commission', and OFSTED monitoring that the targets had actually been met.

I know you want to keep it simple, Body, but is this not a trifle over-egged? or should the massed bands of the Grenadier Guards be hired to accompany Pavarotti, Domingo and Carreras in a vocal celebration of the 300 quid award, just to push the cost of the whole silly exercise up a bit further?

Still, I think I've got the hang of it now. The best strategy for getting a performance award seems to be first of all to send home all the pupils for a year. That way you stay well within budget (the top indicator). Furthermore your pupils score zero in SATs and public examinations first time round, so you then let a few pupils back in each year to ratchet up the test scores, thereby ensuring annual bonuses for at least a decade.

Next, you ply heads with alcohol for three years to make them rolling averages, though they may have to spend their bonus on hangover cures. Finally, you invite the governors, the parents, the thousands of teachers who are livid because they got a zero pay award, the Audit Commission, OFSTED and the Dagenham Girl Pipers to an enormous knees-up to celebrate the deputy head's £300 windfall.

I've got to hand it to you, Body, you've finally cracked the problems of performance-related pay. I suggest you now put your paperette in the filing cabinet and pull the trigger. Or better still, the flush.

30 September 1994

Creating fossilized follies for the future

You have to laugh. The Office for Educational Standards cannot find enough primary inspectors to fillet the thousands of primary schools due for ritual shredding if the target of 20,000 inspections in the next four years is to be met. Excuse me a moment while I pass a couple of sacks of onions across my nostrils in a futile attempt to raise a teardrop at the pickle the Office for Standards in Education finds itself in. It serves them right for killing off the decently professional inspectorate.

Apparently 700 registered primary inspectors have been 'trained' (that means, I presume, transported by train to the brief sojourn in Fawlty Towers that passes for professional inspectorial induction nowadays). Out of these, some 300 have not even bid for a single primary school inspection contract to date.

It is astonishing that OFSTED is hurt and disappointed at this slightly less than ecstatic response. What on earth did they expect? You only have to look back to 1992 to see at least one of the reasons why this should have happened. The new-style school inspections are part of what purports to be a free market. Anyone, even a butcher, according to Kenneth Clarke at the time, could inspect a school.

Expensive block adverts in the national and local press were launched, with no expense spared, to recruit a squad of freebooting gung-ho heavies. Even the training of them has now been privatized. The lavish advertising campaign back in July 1992 gloried in the unrestricted entrepreneurial nature of the whole exercise. 'School children need testing. So do schools. Have you the skills to be a school inspector?' ran the headline, alongside a picture of an inspector sitting in a science lab. 'This is a flexible opportunity,' the ads purred on seductively, 'once registered you can tender for as few or as many projects as you wish to take on'.

Just a minute, sunshine. You said it, so why complain if punters decide that, in their case, 'as few as you wish' should equal 'none'? A market is a market. If some certificated Ofstedders are saying: 'Thanks for the badge, but stuff your inspections. I propose instead to make a fortune as a private consultant, squeezing money out of desperate

schools wanting a dummy run before the real thing', then that's the market for you.

Cut to the quick by this snub, OFSTED is writing to all registered primary inspectors who have not put in tenders to find out why. Now I don't want to prejudge the findings, but I suspect it will be a touch difficult to prise out the truth. Not many will confess to being far too busy coining it through private consultancy. Few will admit that they are still in traction, having dislocated their funny bone laughing at the moronic nature of the whole exercise. None will divulge their distaste at the prospect of a week in a seedy guest house with a vanload of retired technology advisers and Mafeking veterans with smelly socks. They will all say they are engrossed elsewhere.

I suspect that one major reason for not tendering is the robotic framework. If you read a few reports it becomes clear how the writing up actually works. In the 493-page OFSTED 'How to gut a school' manual there are two specimen reports. Some of the writers of real-life reports seem merely to have copied these on to their word processor. They then fill in the gaps. Hence the frequency of statements like: 'Standards of achievement in the core subjects are . . . (a) above, (b) below, (c) close to . . . the national average', and 'The quality of education provided is generally. . . (a) good, (b) satisfactory, (c) unsatisfactory'. A chimpanzee could fill in the gaps, and for all I know probably does.

Indeed this latest version of OFSTED officialese, Ofskrit, should now be classified by the United Nations as a separate language in its own right. Then people could put it down on their CV when applying for jobs: 'I speak fluent French, German and Ofskrit'. Ofskrit is certainly a branch of English, but in few other contexts would words like 'satisfactory', 'usually', 'generally' occur with such determined frequency.

I could never cope with having to write Ofskrit. The temptation to put something utterly ridiculous or unexpected in the gaps would be irresistible. It would be great fun to break the mould: 'The management of the school is . . . (a) good, (b) satisfactory, (c) about as well organized as an Italian bus queue', or 'The governors have recently agreed a health policy which . . . (a) covers the field adequately, (b) few of the turnips actually understood, since some governors find Ladybird Book 3 a real challenge, (c) should kill off most of the little sods in Year 10 and cut class sizes to below 30'.

Perhaps some palaeontologist in the ninety-ninth century will dig up the bones of inspectors, carbon-date them, translate the fragments of Ofstrit text discovered alongside the remains, and construct a complete fossil record from the nineteenth century onwards. It will look something like this:

1830s Inspectus Erectus
1870s Inspectus Terrorus
1920s Inspectus Blandus (missing link)
1950s Inspectus Sensibilis
1960s Inspectus Progressivus
1970s Inspectus Trendius
1980s Inspectus Legalisticus

1992 Inspectus Clarkius Extinctus
1994 Inspectus Utterly Ludicrus

In 1996 the fossil record ends. No further bones are known. The only clue about the demise is a fragment of parchment found at a burial ground, written in what is believed to be ancient Ofskrit. It states that the species 'usually, generally and satisfactorily' disappeared up its own rhetoric.

14 October 1994

Quality fetishists are streets ahead

There is exciting news for those interested in the great kwality in education fetish. Brace yourselves, kwality fans everywhere. The British Standards award for kwality, BS 5750, has now been renamed BS EN ISO 9001. There, I thought that would shock you.

Not many people know that. I didn't know it, and what is more I was blissfully happy in my ignorance. Personally I do not care whether it is renamed KRAPP 22 or DIAL 999. Somehow the sheer meaninglessness of BS EN ISO 9001 says it all. Roll it round the tongue. Savour its utter pointlessness.

Kwality will never be the same again, thanks to good old BS EN ISO 9001. I wonder what you have to do to get BS EN ISO 9002. If you are ever in Florence, take a close look at Michelangelo's David. He has now got BS EN ISO 9001 stamped on his leg, and he is all the better for it.

It is very difficult to challenge the particular view of quality in education, with its emphasis on structures, that has recently become predominant. If you do, then you run the risk of being accused of favouring the slipshod and the substandard. Your friends start to look uncomfortable, as if proximity to a heretic might deny them a place in heaven. Conformists that most of us are, we tend to ride with it. 'We've set up a quality assurance committee,' someone said to me recently. 'We had to. You can't really afford not to have one, can you?'

As a result, form takes precedence over content. I know of institutions that are bristling with quality assurance structures, that win medals and badges for them, but whose actual work is shoddy. There is almost an inverse relationship between the stridency with which institutions scream about kwality, and the real quality of what goes on there. The top outfits are usually relaxed about it, and the naff ones keep telling you how much of it they have got.

If you are in the first year of your inheritance you can go to any number of expensive conferences on the subject. Lectures are given by managers, directors, deans and controllers of quality. There is a professor of constructive capitalism in a university in Texas, so no doubt there is a professor of kwality as well somewhere (don't write in, stay well hidden).

It makes you wonder whether this whole kwality push is in part driven by the miserable shortage of proper resources. Schools have been spending little money on books lately and premises are shabby. Some £4 billion is needed to bring school buildings up to scratch. As book and equipment stores diminish, teacher redundancies abound, class sizes go up and the fabric of education deteriorates. It is almost as if government pressure to acquire and display the badges and trappings of quality has become a substitute for these essentials, a desperate attempt to reassure the public that all is well.

In September, when the Prime Minister went to South Africa, the following report appeared in *The Times*: 'John Major delighted pupils and teachers at the school when he unveiled a fully equipped library filled with literature provided by the British Government.' No one would begrudge the gesture. South Africa is emerging from turmoil and children need all the help they can get. But it would be nice if he unveiled a few fully equipped government-provided school libraries here as well, in places other than city technology colleges and schools that have opted out.

It is not clear what the South Africans were given. Does *The Times* report of the 'library filled with literature provided by the British Government' mean that they supplied the library or the literature? If they provided the literature, then this could explain what happened to all the surplus copies of that ludicrous Government anthology of great literature for key stage 3, the one that contained three lines of Chaucer and half a poem by Shelley 'n Keats. Perhaps it was spare copies of the Parent's Charter, or worse, that extremely thin volume *The Educational Thoughts of Kenneth Clarke*. If so, should we not be exporting this stuff to our enemies, rather than our friends? And will it do anything other than cure insomniacs?

Anyway, to get back to the quality issue, it is high time we had a proper award for real quality in education, for the things that really matter in school. See how many of these searching questions you can answer in the affirmative:

1 During break, is coffee stirred with a pencil or a Biro, rather than a spoon?
2 Does the caretaker really run the school?
3 Does the deputy head play old Beatles songs in assembly, frantically trying to pretend there's a coherent message in the lyrics?
4 Is the staff car park full of N-registered Ford Escorts?
5 Has someone written graffiti in staff toilets saying things like 'Raise the national IQ, kill an OFSTED lay inspector', or 'Just because you're paranoid, it doesn't mean the buggers aren't really out to get you'?
6 Can at least half the staff play bridge and mark books at the same time?
7 Is the head planning to retire early, buy a boat, and call it *Lump Sum*?
8 Has some joker piled a stack of national curriculum documents from floor to ceiling?
9 Does the school blow its total INSET budget on a weekend in a seaside hotel?
10 Is the staffroom copy of the school's development plan used as a teapot stand?

If you can truthfully answer 'Yes' to all 10 quality questions, then congratulations. Your school has real style. You have now qualified to have BS EN ISO 9001 stamped on your bum.

28 October 1994

What a carry-on in the wee small hours

'The Office for Standards in Education has produced a short video to reassure schools due to be inspected. It is to be screened on Channel 4 at 4 am on December 6, and costs £30 from OFSTED, Room 11/3,

Elizabeth House, York Road, London SE1 7PH.' I know that life often imitates art, but I found this news item in *The Times Educational Supplement* barely credible. How can I be expected to produce a piece of fortnightly lunacy on the back page of *The TES* when OFSTED is capable of trumping every ace?

I wouldn't have dared write a *Carry on OFSTED* film script. It makes you wonder if the whole thing is a spoof. Have they really produced a video? Will it really be shown on Channel 4 at that peak hour of 4 am, when every teacher is glued to the television screen? Does it really cost £30? And is there such a room as 11/3?

It is all true. There is a video. It will indeed be transmitted to all six viewers who tune to Channel 4 at 4 am. Though you could rent much more interesting feature films, like *The Three Stooges Inspect a School* and *Frankenstein becomes a Lay Inspector* for a fraction of the cost, you can, if you so wish, squander 30 quid on the OFSTED masterpiece. Room 11/3 is real enough and can be found between rooms 11/2 and 11/4.

Fortunately I have managed to obtain a copy of the *Carry on OFSTED* film script.

'Stand by everybody. *Carry on OFSTED* video. Take 1. Action!'

[*Chariots of Fire* music. A squad of amateur inspectors is seen jogging along the beach. Two fall down, several run into the sea by mistake. Three lay inspectors in bath chairs are counting grains of sand. Only inspector to spot film crew comes over to speak to camera.]

Inspector: 'Hello. I'm your friendly OFSTED amateur inspector and I'm going to show you that there's nothing to be afraid of when we come to your school.'

[Cut to picture of fluffy kitten.]

'We just want to inspect what you're doing and there's no need to worry, because we're all highly trained.'

[Cut to seaside hotel. Close-up of sign saying FAWTY TOWRES. Enter Kenneth Williams and Sid James.]

Sid James: 'If that berk mentions test scores one more time, I'll ram 'is league table right up 'is bleeding SAT Tracker.'

Kenneth Williams: 'Oooh, stop messing about Sid. 'E's only doing 'is job, though 'e's a bit below the national average if you ask me.'

[Enter well-proportioned Pinewood starlet.]

Sid James: 'Cor blimey. Look at the performance indicators on 'er. No wonder they call 'er a lay inspector. Geddit?'

[Camera returns to friendly amateur OFSTED inspector, who is unaware he is now on camera and is seen scratching his bum.]

Amateur inspector: 'Er. So you see, there is nothing to be afraid of. No need for any of this (close-up of Librium tablet), nor this (close-up of brandy bottle), nor this (shot of headteacher plummeting off roof of school). We're really your friends.'

[Close-up of piranha fish.]

[Cut to school scene. Close-up on door with 'Headteacher' written on it. Hattie Jacques is seen at her desk with an embroidered motto saying 'St Satan's – *Semper toppus of leagus*' on the wall behind her.]

Hattie Jacques: 'Ah, do come in gentlemen. Tea anybody?'

Sid James [sipping and spitting out tea]: 'Cor blimey, what a load of wee wee. This horse should be shot. Definitely below the national average I shall 'ave to say in my report.'

[Enter one of Her Majesty's Inspectors, looking furtive, clutching briefcase marked 'HMI'.]

HMI: 'It's terrible. [Looks anxiously over his shoulder.] You know, I'm one of the last real HMI left, the others have all gone now since inspection was privatized (bursts into tears). It never used to be like this, with this performance indicator rubbish and "below the national average", "above the national average" and all that meaningless garbage. But there are only a hundred and odd real HMI left now, and we've got to supervise all this amateurish tripe. I can't sleep at night. [Shouts of 'Get him off the set, quick!' and 'Who let him out?'] I can't even tell anybody how awful it is because I've signed the Official Secrets Act. And . . . aaaaaaaargh!.'

[A sack marked OFSTED is thrown over his head and he is dragged off the set struggling and kicking. Camera returns to out-of-focus shot of friendly amateur inspector's left ear.]

Amateur inspector: 'So you see, there's nothing to be afraid of. If you're a big school, just pay cash and we'll all be happy. [Close-up of piles of tenners being put into plain brown envelopes.] And if you're a small school, you'll have no bother at all. There's no money in it, so we won't even put in a tender.' [Shot of staff of small school gleefully spending inspection money in village pub.]

Cast	
Pantomine horse	John Patten (front)
	Kenneth Clarke (back)
Inspector Ivor Briefcase	Kenneth Williams
Inspector Randy Groper	Sid James
Miss Apprehension	Hattie Jacques
Lay Inspectors	Stan Laurel and Oliver Hardy
Butcher	Kenneth Clarke
Gaffer	John Major
Best Boy	Kenneth Clarke

Financed by OFFRIP Costumes by OFFAL Produced by OFFTHEWALL 'Well Below the National Average' Productions Inc.

11 November 1994

Look on my works, ye mighty, and despair

From time to time human achievement seems to reach its pinnacle. There are rare moments in our lives when we are privileged to witness pure genius – Hamlet's soliloquy, Pavarotti singing Puccini's *La Bohème*, Pele playing football for Brazil in the 1970s.

There was, for me, a moment last week when all previous instances of supreme human endeavour paled. I had the privilege of experiencing perfection, the ultimate example of the immaculate. Alongside it Shakespeare, Pavarotti and Pele appeared shoddy. I read a pile of papers about National Vocational Qualifications.

Now I don't want you going out and doing the same thing without clearance from your GP that you are in robust health and that your cardiovascular system can cope with the ecstasy. Reading about NVQs is only for the comprehensively fit person. This Rembrandt of rubbish, this Beethoven of Bakerspeak, this Einstein of eyewash, is not for anyone who is frail or of a nervous disposition.

Don't get me wrong. I am not against vocational education, quite the reverse. Nor do I break into a cold sweat at the prospect of analysing human performance, or indeed at the notion of 'competence' or 'performance'. It is just that when NVQs are written up in the full glory of triply distilled Bakerspeak, the mechanical dreariness is unparalleled. Hence the widespread belief that NVQ stands for Not Very Quotable.

Some people believe that the NVQ 'competency' approach should be imposed on the training of the teaching profession. If you wonder what this would mean, then consider some of the gems in the NVQ-style teaching certificates for teachers in further and adult education. These documents are already saturated with 'element codes', 'range indicators', 'negotiated evidence', and 'performance/product' evidence. Confused? You soon will be.

Take 'competence element' 3.1 of one document, for example. Candidates must 'deliver a programme of learning sessions'. Come again, competence element 3.1? Is this what we traditionalists used to call 'teach'? Will the National Union of Teachers now be renamed the National Union of Deliverers of Learning Sessions, or, if we were so foolish as to saddle the teaching profession with this tosh, the appropriately termed NUDLS? Will staff rooms echo with banter like, 'It's OK for you, but I've got to deliver a programme of learning experiences to Darren Rowbottom this afternoon', as oodles of noodles set about their daily task?

In this fantastic world, where teachers – pardon me, noodles – are seen as Thunderbirds, 'range statements' are defined as 'contexts in which the individual is expected to achieve the standard' on dozens of 'performance criteria'. Reading this mind-numbing accumulation of hundreds of performance criteria is like wading neck-deep through treacle. What on earth does this typical example mean, ignoring the grammatical error 'Referral is conducted in a constructive and sensitive manner which is supportive of the learner and their learning objectives'? We noodles have a right to know.

However, I don't want to be sniffy about it, so I offer this set of NVQ performance criteria for my 'Thunderbirds Are Go' Diploma of Noodling. I hope NVQ fans will not think I am trying to teach my grandmother to suck eggs, or rather, in NVQ-speak, 'deliver a programme of learning experiences to parents' immediate female ancestor within the range statement pertaining to the acquisition of the performance skill of drawing the contents of hard-shelled reproductive bodies into the mouth by inhalation and the force of suction'.

NVQ Noodling Unit 999, Element MADCAP 1b, 'Use the Blackboard'

Candidate's performance criteria:
- ❑ picks up stick of chalk of desired colour;
- ❑ breaks it in two, if whole stick;
- ❑ accurately judges distance between self and blackboard;
- ❑ advances purposefully towards blackboard, avoiding loose bags and coats on floor;
- ❑ successfully selects empty space on blackboard;
- ❑ prepares to face class, first discreetly checking flies or blouse buttons;
- ❑ asks class current calendar date;
- ❑ checks answer in personal diary;
- ❑ writes date on blackboard, accurately spitting on sleeve and erasing any errors.

Knowledge evidence required:
- ❑ how to hold stick of chalk (knowledge of three different grips required, including Steinberg's Three-fingered Backhand);
- ❑ where blackboard is located (10 minutes allowed for search);
- ❑ which pocket contains personal diary (half an hour allowed for search);
- ❑ compass-bearing and national grid reference of own location relative to blackboard;
- ❑ name of the last-but-one Secretary of State (not related to blackboard expertise, but only way Clarkie will ever be remembered).

Range statements.
- ❑ Resources available: blackboard, sleeve, saliva, stick of chalk, flies, blouse, emergent human learning receptacles (pupils).
- ❑ Expected ways of working: health and safety (no inaccurate gobbing on sleeve), equal opportunities (any pupil to be permitted to gob on own sleeve and erase errors), appeals procedures (pupils not allowed to gob on sleeve offered right of appeal), confidentiality (pupils permitted opportunity to gob on sleeve anonymously).

Any comments on the proposal to impose NVQ procedures on the education and training of the noodling profession should be sent to Captain Thunderbird, NVQ House, Naff Enterprises Inc, Drowning-in-the-Jargon, Tillit, Herts.

25 November 1994

6

Mad Curriculum Disease

One of Kenneth Baker's worst legacies was the most complex national curriculum and testing programme in Europe. We moved from extreme permissiveness to extreme prescription within a year. Such was the Government's suspicion of teachers that the first version of the curriculum was spelled out in minute detail in dozens of files and booklets. European educators looked on in astonishment, as they were trying to simplify what they prescribed while we sailed past them in the opposite direction. Large numbers of teachers began to suffer from what I often referred to as 'Mad curriculum disease'.

A ghost still full of beans

One of my greatest pleasures, as a youth, was to act in the school play. We would stay on after school and live through some monumental drama, week upon week, until we all knew every word off by heart, irrespective of the part we were playing. To this day I can recall the chilling experience of seeing Macbeth confronted by the ghost of Banquo. I was reminded a couple of weeks ago of how the poor beggar must have felt, watching someone he thought had passed on actually appear before his eyes.

There I was, innocently watching the news, barely sober after a six week celebration at Mr Bun having finally departed from the DES, leaving only the faintest whiff of scorched Brylcreem, the first, and hopefully last hologram to be Education Secretary, when Old Smarmy Boots rushed before the cameras in the yard of the first opted-out school. It was only catatonic shock that prevented me leaping up and declaiming like the demented Macbeth, 'Hence horrible shadow! Unreal mockery, hence!'

Not that I am opposed to these photo-opportunities, you understand. After all, it was an everyday occurrence at my school for us to stroll across the playground holding hands with a Cabinet Minister and the headmaster wearing his gown, and smiling at the assembled press. What shocked me was the thought that Bun might go on appearing in school yards and classrooms to the end of time, gibbering on about the success of his Education Act. Perhaps in 50 years' time the BBC will be cashing in on the nostalgia for it with *Dad's Army*, the story of a few intrepid, if comical, elderly licensed teachers, and *'Allo 'Allo*, a series about teachers imported from France trying to control 3C on a wet Friday afternoon.

It was no surprise to discover that one of Bun's first moves as Conservative Party chairman was to hire the marketing firm which had been responsible for relaunching a well-known brand of baked beans, to revamp the Government's image. I always thought his style was more suited to selling beans than nurturing the nation's youth. Apparently his and their first job is to find a new logo for the Government, to replace the torch symbol they nicked from the National Union of Teachers, a few years ago. I suggest a great big bean. It would commemorate Bun's mercifully brief sojourn in education and the flatulence that accompanied it, and he would go down in history as Bun the Bean.

Most of the subject reports for the national curriculum which have appeared so far seem to incorporate some of the best classroom practice of recent years. My worry, like that of other teachers, is that there has not been enough time to plan, that the money for all the necessary resources may not be provided, and that the demands of testing and the sheer volume of cumulative requirements might between them screw the whole thing up. I am already getting a bit neurotic, with any class I teach, about which of the attainment targets I might have covered.

Last week I was playing a game with a class of five-year-olds who had just started school. They had to point to their eyes, their nose or whatever, when I mentioned these, and then they could move to 'Cleverland'. Normally it would have been the sort of harmless game one plays with children of five without further ado, but this time it was a special occasion. I had just 'delivered' my first piece of the national curriculum, science national curriculum attainment target three, 'Processes of Life', level one, ('know parts of the body'), to be precise. Only 9,999 to go, or rather 'be delivered', must keep up the beans jargon.

It occurred to me that there could be an economical, (or is it 'cost effective'?) way of delivering the beans, as they no doubt say in Bun's office nowadays. What I needed was a single inspiration, some monumentally comprehensive but brief event, which would wipe out the whole of the primary national curriculum in one fell swoop. Suddenly I had it. All we needed to do was sing my old childhood favourite. 'The Grand Old Duke of York.' It was brilliant and will save me hours.

Since it is a poem, that covers English, and if you sing it as well then you have taken care of music. The rest of the national curriculum goes like this.

Oh, the Grand Old Duke of York.
(history)
He had 10,000 men;
(maths)
He marched them up to the top of the hill,
Then he marched them down again
(PE and geography)

And when they were up they were up,
And when they were down they were down)
(Science, – well, it included 'measurement and observation')
And when they were only half-way up,
They were neither up nor down.

The relevance of this last couplet may be obscure but I am calling it design and technology on the grounds that business studies is subsumed under the design-and-technology heading and the two lines sum up beautifully the state of many British businesses. If you are in any doubt you can always get the class to type the poem on the word processor and then log it in under the information technology attainment target of the design-and-technology label.

The children then paint a picture of it, so that takes care of art, and all nine subjects are under your belt. Secondary teachers can ask the class to translate it into French, thus nailing modern languages at the same time. So there you are, the whole national curriculum in just a single lesson. It's the absolute beans.

22 September 1989

In search of a true explorer

It did take a very long time for the membership of the national curriculum geography committee to be announced. The reason for this delay, I am told, was that Mr Bun wanted an explorer to chair it, but could not find one.

Now this does raise several very interesting issues, not the least of which is that it is hardly surprising that Bun could not turn up a real live explorer. If there is one human group that is not sitting in an armchair clutching a mug of hot cocoa, waiting for Bun to phone, it is the genus explorers. It ought to have been screamingly obvious that real explorers are out exploring, so head for the North Pole if you want one.

The thought of Bun wading neck deep up the Limpopo, complete with pith helmet, pursued by a dozen camera crews, cracked me up: 'Dr Livingstone, I presume, would you like to chair my geography committee?' Perhaps he disguised himself as Kenneth 'the Eagle'

Baker in the last winter Olympics in the faint hope of finding a curriculum minded explorer up in the Arctic wastes. I suppose we are lucky the geography committee is not being chaired by some bewildered Eskimo.

The main question it raised for me, however, was about the nature of professionalism. There is a tendency nowadays for some politicians to assume that people professionally involved in an enterprise are not capable of considering wider issues, belong to a self-protecting interest group, cannot empathize with the non-expert, and are incapable of objective judgement. Yet many true experts have none of these faults, even if some do, and it is wrong to assume that an amateur is always needed for wise decisions to be reached.

Another aspect of professionalism under threat in education is over the matter of school support services.

Though usually referred to as 'jobs' rather than 'professions', occupations such as school caretaker, secretary, cleaner and so on have often been carried out according to the best tenets of professionalism, with complete commitment to the school community.

The provision of contracted privatized service could offer a cheaper and more efficient service to schools once they have local financial management and are able to choose their supplier. It might also, I fear, jeopardize that dedicated commitment by on-site caretakers and cleaners, who have often built up over many years that strong sense of devotion to duty which is a hallmark of good professionalism.

In one area which has already set up such a service the dangers are clear to see. Caretakers have been given cars, mobile phones, a written contract and several schools to patrol. Newly Yuppified they cruise round the countryside opening the first schools on their list as early as 6 a.m. on the ground that the contract only says 'unlock the schools', it doesn't say at what time. When a pupil is sick in a classroom and the head rings up Alpha Delta Four on his mobile phone, the reply comes that there is nothing about cleaning up vomit in the contract. Consequently heads and teachers are mopping up, cleaning out swimming pools and doing several jobs formerly undertaken without demur by their local on-site caretaker.

If there is one notion, however, which chills the blood so far as professionalism is concerned, it is that of 'awareness'. There is so much for teachers to cover nowadays that the universal answer is the 'awareness' course. Next time a surgeon advances towards you in quest of your appendix ask him whether he has been on an awareness course or actually knows what he is doing.

I remember taking part in a long ashen-faced discussion a few years ago when 'special educational needs' became a buzzword. Should we put on courses for specialists so that they could become trainers of their colleagues, or ought we to mount awareness courses for those who confessed ignorance? We preferred the trainers' course, but the local authority wanted an awareness course. We called it a 'training awareness' course to please everyone.

The themes for awareness rain down: the demands of the 1988 Act, plus the need to be aware of the powers of governing bodies, the views of employers. Teachers wake up in the middle of the night shouting 'Leave me alone. I'm aware, I'm aware'.

I watched a news item on television about an education train that cruises round Wales taking children out on field trips. It was a brilliant idea. We could use it for awareness courses: 'The 10:15 awareness train is about to depart on platform six, calling at special needs, pupil assessment, swimming pool maintenance, cleaning up litter, and all stops to local financial management.' The train driver could go on to chair the national curriculum geography committee.

19 May 1989

Who put the ass in assessment?

There has been a great deal of public and press concern that the new ailment which has been found in cattle could be caught by humans. The symptoms are unsteady gait and uncontrolled lassitude. A related form of the illness has now been detected in teachers.

I refer, of course, to Mad Curriculum Disease, the symptoms of which are unsteady gait and uncontrolled laughter.

I first realized I had caught Mad Curriculum Disease when I noticed people giving me strange looks as I lurched around unsteadily while laughing uproariously at my latest mailing from the School Examinations and Assessment Council. If you have not already received your *Guide to Teacher Assessment* packs A, B and C, then get hold of these three gems quickly.

They don't actually cure Mad Curriculum Disease, but they do confirm whether or not you have got it.

Take the first of the three exceedingly glossy brochures in your right hand, open it at the first page where Philip Halsey, chairman and chief executive, has his cheery 'welcome aboard' statement and progress through at a steady pace, deciding at the bottom of each page whether to laugh or cry. I decided to laugh, Phil, that's why I am currently in the Mad Curriculum Disease isolation ward.

The doctors tell me that, when they first brought me in here, I was not sure whether I had been reading about measuring children or measuring curtains. The first rib-ticklers were the various checklists. Honestly, Phil, I couldn't keep a straight face. From the moment you defined the word 'recently' for me, just in case its meaning had eluded me over the years, I was doubled up. The problem was that I couldn't think of any serious answers to the checklist questions. For example, in reply to the item, 'Was the child puzzled, worried?' I wrote. 'No, but I was'.

Next, as instructed, I turned to Chapter 2 on 'Test anxiety'. When I read your question, 'Which tasks might make it necessary for a teacher to disguise the intention to assess children?' it cracked me up again. Do you have any cute tips on actual disguises, Phil? Would it fool them if I dressed up as Santa Claus and went in saying, 'Ho, ho, ho, everybody, look what Father Christmas has brought you to celebrate the middle of February, a sack full of standard assessment tasks'?

I was, by the way Phil, immensely grateful for the section headed 'problems'. I am glad you pointed out for me 'Children do not progress at the same rate', as I would never have spotted this. Similarly, there was the helpful bit which said that 'the children may "run away" with or prematurely complete the activity'. Mine just ran away with it, Phil, muttering, 'Why do we have to do all this, we're only seven?' or 'Bugger this for a game of soldiers', and haven't been seen since.

When I reached the section that asks whether children were frequently absent, I had to report that mine were now permanently absent, so I turned, as instructed, to Chapter 7 and the tips on how to deal with absentees. I must admit, Phil, I was a bit confused here, because your advice says, 'The safest course with such children may be to increase the frequency of assessment rather than take short-cuts in curriculum delivery'.

I don't want to appear churlish, but my problem is this: they're not actually here, Phil, so it is not easy to test them more frequently.

I'm afraid the Mad Curriculum Disease struck me again and I was left pounding the floor helplessly with mirth.

In any case, you know me. Would I take a short-cut delivering the curriculum? What with the one-way system round here nowadays and the van reluctant to start on these cold mornings, it's bad enough delivering the milk, let alone the curriculum.

In the same section you will recall, you ask whether 'children became obsessed with your record book'. Mine did, Phil, I'm afraid. Several followed me around all day trying to grab it, and one actually ate it. That solved the problem you raise under 'Clipboards and checklists', when you ask if it is possible to 'minimize the intrusiveness of the device'.

Incidentally, Phil, I am very worried about all the reporting and recording of this caper. You know where you say 'Teachers do not need reminding that planning is essential. But they may need reminding that it requires time' – well thanks again for the reminder, you're a pal. However, I did feel a teensy bit overwhelmed by all the pages of coding you suggest, such as: '10 MA 4a – understand and use language associated with angle', '16 SC 3b – be able to measure time with a sundial'. The second of these is quite handy, because we can't afford a clock, but does it have to be so complicated with all these elaborate codes?

Have you any idea how long it is going to take for teachers to fill all this garbage in, Phil, even if they haven't got Mad Curriculum Disease? I gather that your outfit, SEAC, was keen to publish everything by attainment target, but that Ministers wanted something simpler. Good old Ministers, is all I can say.

We have 17 attainment targets in science, 14 in maths, between five and eight in other subjects. Eventually there will be at least 70 of these. Can you tell me, Phil, what would be the point of giving any child, let alone a seven-year-old, a string of 70 digits? And what about those who get 70 grades, all at level 1?

Do you realize that in 1992, when test scores are published, the term 'level 1' will become the new form of playground abuse, replacing 'thickie' and 'spasmo' of yesteryear?

Finally, Phil, thanks for the mnemonic you made up to help me remember everything in your three packs, you know – INFORM, where each letter is the beginning of a telling phrase. The Mad

Curriculum Disease has really got a hold on me now, so I'm not sure I've remembered it all perfectly, but I think it went like this:

Is this monumental bullshit really necessary?
No one who applies it to the letter will remain sane.
For goodness' sake throw it in the bin and start again.
Only 25 hours a day will be needed.
Radically reduce the bureaucracy.
More teachers will quit the profession if you don't.

16 February 1990

SEAC Recorder: Newsletter No. 35

Welcome to Newsletter 35 of the School Examinations and Assessments Council the principle purpose of which, as in the previous 34, is to suggest that we are all one big happy family and that there is nothing nasty about national testing.

Hence the odd bit of Welsh and the many photographs of smiling people holding clipboards and files, clearly having terrific fun.

The only exception is the group captioned 'GCSE examiners marking scripts' showing people sitting round a table covered in test papers. We feature this picture just in case you thought examiners spent their time doing cartwheels.

What is a SAT?

Many teachers have written to SEAC asking if they can see what a Standard Assessment Task (SAT) looks like. There are not many about but one was sighted running across a field near the A1 during that hot spell in July.

As readers will know the purpose of the SATs is to test children's knowledge of the National Curriculum through specially devised tests, usually assessing levels in more than one subject. The results of the pilots have not yet been fully analysed but three consortia were each given a third of the National Debt to try out a few ideas. There is currently a keen debate within the Government about the future of national testing. The two options under careful consideration are (a) to give the whole of the gross national product, over a hundred billion pounds, to the newly formed MFOR (Money For Old Rope) consortium to devise tests for the whole population of the United Kingdom on the whole of human knowledge, or (b) just to say 'bugger it' and carry on as usual.

Below is a level 10 SAT piloted with 14-year-olds under the heading 'Snow Across the Curriculum' with the usual subject codes in brackets (e.g. Ma = maths, Te = technology, Gk = God knows etc.).

Snow across the Curriculum

- ❏ Build an igloo (Te).
- ❏ Measure and weigh it (Ma).
- ❏ Write a poem about it (En).
- ❏ Pole vault over it (PE).
- ❏ Melt it (Sc).
- ❏ Say 'Merde, mon igloo est disparu' (ML).

Sop for the Welsh

Pwyllgor Ymgyngh orol dros Cgmru. (This can be translated as: 'Up yours Dai bach, the Government won't listen to you either'.)

Changing faces

Mr Silas Wordgrind, formerly copy-writer of Opaque Bulletins Inc, has joined SEAC as Head of Global Communications. His job is to make sure that SEAC newsletters are jargon-free.

He is delighted with his new appointment and has already committed himself to keeping pedagogical operatives aware-briefed on assessment-oriented decision-making situations.

The Secretary of State has announced three new appointments to the important SEAC Committee committee, which receives minutes from the other 78 SEAC committees, including the powerful Who-Created-All-This-Bloody-Stupid-Bureaucracy Committee.

So we welcome Colonel Adam Smith-Rightwinger, who fought at Mafeking with the Coldstream Guards, Ivor Cheek, principal of Budleigh Salterton City Technology College, and Bess, one of the Queen's corgis.

1988 Act made clear

Many teachers have written to SEAC asking about Section 5(3) of the 1988 Act which states: 'No course of study hereinafter designated as authenticated thereunder shall be provided therewithout by an outside person for pupils of compulsory school age unless approved by the aforementioned Secretary of State'.

In this section:

- ❑ 'Outside person' means a person outside, i.e. not inside.
- ❑ 'an' is the indefinite article when used before a vowel.
- ❑ 'age' means how old you are, as in 'I am 10 years of age.'

Who does what?

The DES requires SEAC to consult NCC as well as CGLI, NFER, BTEC, BBC, ITV, LBW and C&A about GCSE, CPVE, A and AS and SATs (in Wales TAFFs) based on TGAT.

Subsequently the CBI and TUC comment with the DTI and DOE on training issues which are then conveyed to SEAC and NCC by the GPO. The LEAs report through AMA or ACC to CLEA, except in Yorkshire where they report to EEBYGUM.

Terms explained No. 35

Attainment target: This comes from the two words 'attainment' meaning something you reach, like your peak, the sky or the door, and 'target' which is, according to the Oxford English Dictionary, 'a circular stuffed pad' or something you fire or attempt to hit.

Thus 'attainment target' is reaching a state of feeling stuffed, believing you are shooting at the sky, or attempting to hit your head against a door.

Next month: 'Utterly knackered'.

21 September 1990

The Relapse . . . or Carry On Testing

I was cured. Straight up, I was pronounced completely clear of all Mad Curriculum Disease symptoms, not a twitch, clean bill of health. Then look what happened. I went along to my first SAT training conference and here I am, back in a packed Mad Curriculum Disease isolation ward, alongside all the other participants, lurching round hysterically in my carpet slippers, sniggering uncontrollably.

We inmates now spend most of our day muttering meaningless jargon and filling anything square-shaped with endless ticks and digits. I got put in solitary yesterday for entering a row of twos in Biro on the consultant's check shirt. Apparently I was just jibbering, 'But you're average, man', before they sedated me and put me away for the night.

I knew it had started as soon as I received my briefing pack from the School Examinations and Assessment Council. I would have written to Philip Halsey, the chairman and chief executive of SEAC, thanking him, but it came in a parcel about two inches thick containing somewhere between 200 and 300 photocopied pages of unadulterated bureaucratic twaddle. Honestly, Phil, my finely tuned electronic tripe-detector just emitted a single high-pitched whine before congealing into a shapeless blob of molten metal and plastic.

Perhaps it was because my pack fell open at a wad labelled 'School Assessment Folder Part Seven', which begins with a belter, a comprehension-defying section telling me about the Education (National Curriculum) (Assessment Arrangements for English, Mathematics and Science) Order 1990 and the Education (National Curriculum) (Assessment Arrangements in English, Welsh, Mathematics and Science) (Wales) Order 1990. I wish you had sent me the Welsh version, Phil, it might have been clearer.

This gem is in a section headed 'What you Must Do', which orders me to complete documents A and C. It is written in a cheery tone and says things like, 'You might also find that documents B and D are helpful in completing A and C.' The more the merrier I always say.

What shocked me is that, by the time it got into its stride, this particular text had scaled heights never before attained, even during manned space flight: 'When the results for each girl have been transferred, count up how many girls attained each level, and enter the totals at the right hand side of the form. For each attainment target, profile component and subject, check that the totals for D, N, W, 1, 2 and 3 add up to the total number of girls in Year 2. For Ma 6 the totals for D, N, 1, 2 and 3 should add up to the total number of girls in Year 2. Repeat the process for boys.' That's top drawer, Phil, world class.

Trying to remind myself that this was all about seven-year-old children, not someone's plan to forecast eight score draws on next Saturday's football pools, I turned next to the Teacher's Book. May I suggest a government health warning here Phil, saying something like, 'Warning: Opening this book can cause a fatal bout of uncontrolled mirth'?

Take for example Ma 1, to use the bizarre language of these things, which is the first maths task. My instructions say, 'Place all forty counters in two unequal piles. Ask the children which of the two piles of counters would make the longer straight line if the counters were arranged end to end'. No sweat, Phil. Thirty-nine in one pile, one in the other. That should bump up the school's batting average in the league table.

Off now to Sc 5, or science as you and I used to call it when life was simpler. This one is about 'Things we throw away', and I am instructed, 'Ask the children to tell you about the kinds of things that they would expect to find in a dustbin/waste bin/refuse sack'. No problem round here. The bins are so full of SEAC documents there's no room for much else.

English is equally rich. En 1 (you can be proud of me, even with Mad Curriculum Disease I still remember the code book) instructs me to 'Plan some games that require children to give each other instructions'. One crisp suggestion is to blindfold children and then get them to give each other instructions about how to reach an object. Thanks, Phil, you're a pal. I can just see it: 'Left a bit, right a bit, no not there you fool, come back, A-a-a-r-g-h'.

Has anyone at SEAC the slightest understanding of the reality of trying out all these capers with a classroom full of seven-year-old livewires? I can just see the people wandering round with their clipboard giving meaningless marks based on eavesdropping on casual conversations during an unspecified game. I tried out poker. Apart from losing about 20 quid it was not too bad, Phil, but how do you score, 'Hit me for three', 'See your 10 and raise you 10', or 'I'm all cleaned out, pass me another Heineken'?

Incidentally, I had a pantomime with Level 2, Part D on En 1; you remember, the bit about assessing 'talk with the teacher'. I was not sure how many qualified for Level 2 in the section where I have to 'Observe children who show, by their facial expression or posture, that they are listening to what you say'. Darren sat throughout my talk with his tongue out, Melanie stood on her head, and Gary held up a sheet of paper on which he had written 'Artistic impression – minus 1.5'. Algernon Fforbes-Ffrench is cross-eyed, so I was not sure whether he was looking at me or the radiator.

Finally the documentation. The sad thing is, Phil, that a few of these tasks would actually be quite interesting to do. Weed out the dafter ones, cut back on the paperwork, and it might be a runner. But the page upon page of squared and lined paper, the sheet after sheet, row upon row, column after column, are simply too much for seven-year-olds, too much for their teachers and the degree of detail is way over the top.

All this is screamingly obvious now, let alone after this year's pilots. The whole programme in its present form is crackers, mad, loony, screwy, potty, completely nuts. It reads more like a script for the latest British comedy *Carry On Testing*. Do we really have to put schools through the wringer in the summer term with the inevitable turmoil that will produce?

The saddest thing of all is that when heads and others have been to their training sessions, they and thousands of teachers who are perfectly competent at their job will feel that they must be failures because (a) the whole exercise is so complex and detailed, and (b) the documentation is crippling.

It will be the fault of the system not of themselves, but the Mad Curriculum Disease isolation wards will still be full to overflowing.

22 February 1991

No sex please, we're squeamish

I cringed when I read about the Family Planning Association workbook on sex education for primary school children. As a member of a generation raised on 'thingies', 'whatsits' and a host of other euphemisms, the current fad for being explicit about 'you know what' is a complete toe curler.

It is all very well for the FPA to adopt what in other circumstances might be called a 'let it all hang out' approach, but when it comes to their cheerful recommendation that the teacher should play an information game, in which seven to eleven-year-old children ask questions about orgasms, then include me out, as Sam Goldwyn once said. Leave that sort of thing till later, and then to experts with degrees in orgasmology who can brass-neck it, not to my hung up generation whose faces glow like illuminated tomatoes at the mere mention of such thingies.

I know this is all irrational and one should be able to take a mature and dispassionate view of the topic, but there are some things a decently shy sort of chap cannot do for Britain, and this is one of them. I will have a bash at teaching subjects I have to mug up the night before, topics I do not particularly enjoy, or even the National Curriculum technology syllabus. I will fly the Union Jack to please John Patten, or read pamphlets written by the Centre for Policy Studies. But I will not ram bananas into condoms on a Friday afternoon.

One exercise for four to seven-year-olds creased me. 'Materials: large pieces of paper, felt tips, Sellotape, labels with names of body parts including sexual and reproductive organs'. You then divide the children into groups of four to six and ask them to find one member of each group to lie down while the others draw round them. Next they have to label the drawing of the corpse. I am afraid that in my class it would be with labels marked 'thingy', 'dangling thingy' and 'naughty thingies'. It certainly beats anything the National Curriculum Council dreamed up.

Three years ago the Government ran a teacher recruitment campaign under the slogan 'It's quite a challenge making fractional distillation more interesting than sex'. Not if it becomes too matter-of-fact an element of the official school curriculum it isn't. If you want to reduce the birthrate dramatically, then set up a National

Curriculum sex education subject panel, presumably making it a 'Cor!' subject, produce a ring-bound folder (in beetroot red please) with a 10-level syllabus, and then put it through the House of Commons and the Lords. Mind you, in view of some of the funny goings-on in high places, goodness knows what would emerge from that particular palace. I can't wait to see the SATs. What is certain is that any over officialization and bureaucratization of sex education would eliminate the human race within a generation.

Perhaps we of the coy brigade could be put on such a subject panel. Level one could be 'know about thingies', level two could be 'how's your father?', level three 'the role and function of the whatsit', level four 'nudge nudge'. At GCSE pupils could write about rumpty-tumpty and answer questions requiring them to label the naughty bits in rude pictures. Eventually I can imagine the ultimately minimalist BA finals examination philosophy question, which would simply ask 'Know what I mean?'. At least there would be little argy bargy from the right-wing think tanks about stretching bright pupils by moving them up the levels faster, and taking the SATs early in private schools.

Despite my personal embarrassment at the thought of having to teach it, however, I am all in favour of children learning about sex from skilful teachers who know how to treat it appropriately. Sex education has been well taught in many primary and secondary schools. The BBC and other agencies have produced coherent sensible programmes tailored to the age group, with topics covered in a sensitive manner. At its best, teaching programmes have been devised at local level by those committed to doing it well, and parents have been fully involved, often seeing videos and discussing the issues themselves at parents' meetings.

This means that steps must be taken to cope with the squirm factor, both from parents and from teachers like me. Children can be hopelessly ignorant about sex if left to playground gossip about which thingy does what. The social, family and moral aspects of sex, as well as the biological facts, do need to be learned, partly in the home and partly in school, if teenage pregnancies are to be reduced and ignorance about AIDS and other matters overcome. I once did a study of the use of broadcasts in small schools. One head said that some parents did not want topics like AIDS to be covered, yet the school was near a park where discarded needles from drug addicts lay in the grass where children played.

Sex education is normally the one subject which does not include discovery learning. This whole hoo-ha reminds me of the story told about the primary pupil who was asked to find out how children were born and write it up for homework. First he asked his older sister. She told him that children were bought at Woolworths. He had never actually seen a baby counter at Woolworths, but in true primary homework tradition he wrote it down.

Next he asked his mother. She told him that babies were found under gooseberry bushes. He duly recorded this evidence. Finally granny was quizzed. Deeply embarrassed she murmured something about babies being delivered in a Gladstone bag. He had no idea what such a container was, but he faithfully noted it down.

The following day he handed in his homework, which began, 'After exhaustive empirical investigation I have managed to ascertain that there has been no sexual intercourse in our family for three generations'.

5 November 1993

Get out the shredder, cognitively speaking

From time to time a bureaucracy will send out a document that is so opaque, so laughably incomprehensible, that it deserves to take its place in the *Anthology of Top Grade Tosh*. With the demise of the School Examinations and Assessment Council, there has been an unfilled gap in the market for some months now.

SEAC was capable of producing bullshit of such lyrical perfection, such unadulterated quality, that it was estimated to have a street value of hundreds of pounds per ounce. Thousands of teachers lamented its passing. Where would they get their monthly fix? Whence the origin in future of the tears of helpless mirth that streamed down thousands of cheeks at the peerless drivel that flowed so effortlessly from its printing presses? The nation mourned.

However, as one door closes, another opens to reveal even more treasures. Rest assured, fellow junkies. Regret no longer the passing of

SEAC. The latest purveyor of 100 per cent pure manure is none other than our newish chum the Office for Standards in Education. During the past few weeks, the brains of thousands of heads and teachers have been churned to a fine pulp as they struggled desperately to understand an OFSTED questionnaire entitled *Spiritual, Moral, Social and Cultural Development.*

This absolute belter consists of 22 open-ended questions, written in the kind of language that gets crap a bad name. The sad thing is that the topic is an important one, and the views of teachers should indeed be sought, but not like this. In contrast, the Department for Education has brought out a students' guide to vocational qualifications that is a model of clarity, so there is no reason why centrally-produced documents need defy comprehension.

The obfuscation in the OFSTED questionnaire starts in the very first item: 'With which, if either, are we more concerned, and why: schools' developmental activities, or pupils' developmental state?'. Come again, OFSTED? Who is the 'we', and what can this all mean?

Warming up, the questionnaire continues: 'In relation to pupils' development, what is the balance which society wants schools to adopt between instruction and education?'.

Sorry, I'm not quite with you there either, OFSTED. Bear with me, but I must just pop outside and consult 'society' first, when I can find it, and maybe ponder a little on 'instruction' and 'education'. The shorter questions, like: 'How do cognitive outcomes relate to moral development?' make me feel no better, although I quite like using the word 'cognitive' myself in the right context.

I feel even worse when I wonder what OFSTED is going to do when 25,000 schools reply to 22 open-ended questions, 550,000 freehand replies. We of the Questionnaire Constructors' Union always ask our members to decide one important matter before sending out questionnaires: do you want to read the responses, or shred them?

If you are collecting more than half a million open-ended statements, OFSTED, that will be at least 5,000 to 10,000 hours of reading and analysing time, so I suggest you switch on the shredder now. Just weigh them all and then recycle.

I think I've got the message, however. Questionnaires should be vague, meaningless, frustrating to the recipient, and defy analysis. So I have compiled my very own OFSTED schedule, the Direct Investigation of Rigorous Education (DIRE) Questionnaire, which will shortly wing its way to 25,000 long suffering schools.

General:

1 Do schools exist to educate children, keep teachers off the dole, collect waste paper, either, both, all, or some of these, cognitively speaking, on Fridays?

2 If the school's cultural ethos were left-handed, would the deputy head be an Arsenal supporter, or is it raining?

3 How can schools ensure that pupils use both legs when running, and what is society's attitude to teachers who teach children to hop?

4 Do schools need to instil an understanding of the aerodynamics of the jelly baby and why do gooseberries have those little hairs on them?

5 In not less than 50 pages, comment on the need to reduce the amount of paper used in education nowadays.

Cognitive Brainrot Scale:

Tick one number on the five-point scale from 'strongly agree' to 'strongly disagree':

1 I always sneeze when I wear flip-flops.

2 It was the national curriculum and SATs that made me incontinent.

3 Sheep may safely graze.

4 I cut my toenails with the lawn mower.

5 There's nothing like a cup of cocoa when your wig falls off.

6 My life is so sad I read OFSTED questionnaires for kicks.

7 There are probably no real HMIs left by now, so congrats to Clarkie and Patten for destroying the service.

When you have completed this questionnaire, cut out a circular piece and glue it to your nose. Write on the envelope, in cognitive ink, 'Sender deceased'. Then post what remains of the questionnaire, along with some bird droppings from your school yard, to The White Hot Shredder, OFSTED, Offthewall, Absolutely Offal, Bringback, HMI.

25 March 1994

7

A view from the head

During this whole period of mayhem, head teachers have been under particular strain. Sadly some caved in and had to retire early. Others developed nifty footwork to stay in business. This chapter records some of the outpourings of the world-weary, been-there, seen-it, 'any-chance-of-early-retirement?' heads, as well as the occasional 'new breed' head who, like Winston Smith in Orwell's *1984*, got to love Big Brother, bought the package, and decided to 'deliver the curriculum'.

The bitter end

My Lord Mayor, governors, parents and pupils of the school. This is my final speech day address as Headmaster before my blissfully awaited retirement next Thursday, and, with the memory of 24 years' worth of pure public relations bilge on such occasions behind me, I should like to take the opportunity, on this my last speech day, of saying something more closely approximating to the truth, fortified only by my conscience and a bottle and a half of Niersteiner Spätlese.

This year has been one of what might be called modest achievements here at East Swineshire. The A-level results were quite pathetic, but I should like to congratulate the two pupils who passed. Arnold Sidebottom managed to disengage himself from his girlfriend long enough to notch a couple of grade Es, and Elspeth Sanderson, the school swot, who sadly is unlikely ever to have to disengage herself from anyone, obtained three grade As. As she is the daughter of an architect I can only put it down to a genetic endowment superior to that with which most of the proletariat seated here have saddled their offspring.

Our O-level and CSE results were also dreadful. This may indeed be the consequence of the authority ending its policy of double entry, a dubious process whereby some children were put in for both GCE and CSE in the faint statistical hope that one board or other would temporarily take leave of its senses and give a pass grade. Knowing this authority, I suspect even single entry is in serious jeopardy next year.

Bearing in mind that a thumbprint gets grade 5 at CSE nowadays, and a neat thumbprint grade 4, our special congratulations are due to the six pupils who performed the superhuman feat of obtaining an ungraded CSE. In view of their considerable absences from school during the year, perhaps we can persuade the board to award them a posthumous grade 1 in shopping.

I shall not dwell on games results. Our lack of success on the rugby field can partly be explained by the departure of four of the more psychopathic members of the first XV, and partly by the boys' understandable preference for the vastly superior game of soccer, which could easily be introduced in the school but for the intransigence of our alcohol-crazed old boys' association.

There are one or two staff changes to report. Mr Trubshaw, whom I tried without success to persuade to hang up his chalk at the earliest opportunity, is now taking his disability pension after what the school magazine will call his 'unfortunate accident' outside the school gates, but what I can only describe as a godsend. I should like to congratulate the driver of an unmarked purple van, last seen heading for the motorway at high speed, on both his aim and timing, and assure him that his return would be warmly welcomed any time he would like to reduce still further my somewhat lengthy hit list.

So far as my own successor is concerned, I am delighted to say that my obsequious deputy Grimsdyke, the Uriah Heep of East Swineshire, failed to hoodwink the normally gullible selection committee with his nauseating public deference, and will have to soldier on as deputy in charge of what we jokingly call pastoral care. I see he is not in the hall at this moment, and is no doubt either rounding up absentees in his usual gauleiter manner, or Sellotaping sticks of gelignite to the underside of my chair.

Parents will have noticed that the building has not been decorated for 17 years and we are down to the original cave paintings in places. I can only suggest that you all vote for red telephone boxes in the *Nationwide* poll, so that British Telecom has to sell us its surplus yellow paint as a cheap job lot.

Some parents have been worried about the court judgment on the photocopying of books. The county solicitor assures me that it does not apply to the copying out longhand of set books, so parents engaged in this utterly futile waste of their time need not be anxious. Next year pupils are studying *War and Peace*. If we melted down the tons of precious metal worn around the well-fed necks of the civic dignitaries on the platform we could buy the British Library twice over. Incidentally, I have put the rest of this year's capitation allowance on Silvertown Boy in the 2.30 at Kempton which at 10-1 could provide all the books we ever need.

Finally, a word about Councillor Bentley, my chairman of governors, and his political cronies at County Hall, where in my view the neutron bomb should be tested. It has been an inspiration to work so closely with this reincarnation of Al Capone and his fellow hoods. I should like to wish them all an acute attack of haemorrhoids. Ladies and gentlemen, I invite you to sing the concluding hymn, dedicated to the future of Swineshire's children. Hymn number 236, 'For those in peril'.

6 March 1981

Management by all

'Ah, come in Jenkins. Last day of term, thank goodness. Just popped in to wish me well before you shoot off to the Dordogne or somewhere, have you?'

'Skegness actually, headmaster. No, I was really wanting a word about the new management structure you've just announced for next year.'

'Indeed, indeed. Well, Jenkins, in all modesty I think we can say we're in at the beginning of something really big here. You see, as I explained at the staff meeting, we've been through all that dreary stuff about management by objectives, management by consent, we even tried management by embarrassment at one point, but I am sure that my new concept of "management by all" is most definitely going to set a national trend and really put us on the map.'

'That's what I wanted to talk to you about, headmaster.'

'You see David . . .'

'It's Donald.'

'Of course. You see, Donald, times have changed. When I first came into this great profession of ours it was full of headmasters who were white-haired old gents, distant autocrats in charge of raw beginners. With a much more mature teaching force we must evolve a style of management that is in accord with the times. That is why I have created the largest senior management team in the county, 39 people, a formidable fighting outfit totally dedicated to the successful running of this school. Now are you telling me that my concept of management by all is a bad one?'

'No, headmaster. It's just that I was a bit disappointed at not being a member of the senior management team myself. After all, when I knew that 39 people were going to be in the team I thought I must have a pretty good chance.'

'Well, of course, management by all does not literally mean that absolutely everybody must be among the magic 39.'

'But that's my whole point, headmaster. There are only 40 of us on the staff. I feel humiliated being the only person not in the senior management team. I mean, did it have anything to do with the staff handbook incident?'

'Look Donald, of course I knew that you were the person who wrote "Argentine Ministry of Information" in felt-tipped pen across the front cover of the staffroom reference copy, but I am not a man who bears a grudge for very long.'

'I had hoped for one of the deputy headships, originally, especially after I got my MEd and came top of the county course for potential deputy heads.'

'Yes, but you must not be over-ambitious David, not everyone can be a deputy head in the new structure.'

'Headmaster, there are 16 of them. I knew that I stood no chance for Deputy Head (Curriculum) or Deputy Head (Pastoral Care), but when I did the London Marathon in two and a half hours I thought I must be a certainty for Deputy Head (Staff Jogging).'

'Are you saying that Sanderson is not a good choice for the post?'

'But he's 19 stone and he's never run for a bus. In any case he retires next year. I thought at least I might be considered for one of the head of year group jobs and why was Mrs Appleby preferred to me as sixth form co-ordinator?'

'Mrs Appleby is highly respected by the older children, Donald, as you must know, and she deserves a post which fully utilizes her talent and energy.'

'But we don't even have a sixth form. We're an 11–16 comprehensive.'

'The future, Donald, we must look to the future. Who said that all education was a vision of the future, wasn't it Alvin Toffler?'

'Did he also say why we have to have such bizarre head of department posts?'

'Bizarre? I don't understand. All schools have heads of department.'

'Yes, but who else has a Head of Hidden Curriculum?'

'All the HMI reports say that the hidden curriculum is important, and I am sure that Braithwaite will do an excellent job.'

'But that's because he's pretty hidden himself. He takes three days off every time he has a carpet laid.'

'Look Donald, I can understand your bitterness at being the only person not in the senior management team, but don't you see that you have been hand-picked for a very special role next year?'

'I don't understand, headmaster.'

'For management by all to be effective there has to be someone who is actually managed. I've been grooming you for this, Donald. You are the key person in my new plan. You are what I call the "managee". Keep your nose clean and it could become a scale 4, provided the senior management team agrees, of course.'

23 July 1982

Personal profile

'Ladies and gentlemen, perhaps I can explain briefly why I have called all the fifth-year teachers together for this very important meeting. As you know, we at East Swineshire Comprehensive are ever at the forefront of new developments, and Councillor Bentley, our chairman of governors and a leading local businessman, has asked us to introduce a system of profiling instead of GCE and CSE exams to help employers interviewing school leavers.'

'Excuse me, headmaster, but I thought County Hall statistics showed that the job-getting success rate of our last year's leavers had fallen to minus 20 per cent, because not only did no-one get a job, but 20 per cent actually came back and sat in the bicycle sheds every day.'

'We mustn't be too pessimistic, Mr Stratford. I feel we should recognize the pressure from the business community for profiles instead of exam results, and that is why I propose we scrap GCE and CSE for all our fifth-years and adopt a system of profiling instead.'

'Now we have a lot to do, and you all have in front of you an alphabetical list of our 180 fifth-year pupils, plus the 200 item profile we must complete on each pupil. Now, perhaps I can go through the names one by one and we can discuss each item on the schedule. The first name on our list is Shane Abbott of 5K and the first item on the pupil schedule is 'Can push, pull and lift things'. Any comments please? Yes, Miss Foley.'

'Well, I would tend to rate him a good A on pushing, a middling C on pulling, but only a poorish D on lifting, I'm afraid. I suppose that makes him a B double minus overall.'

'No, I'm sorry Miss Foley, we are not using grades. You will see that we simply have to tick either the "yes" or "no" box by each item, so the question is can Shane Abbott push, pull and lift things, yes or no?'

'Look headmaster, can't we save a lot of time and simply tick all 200 "no" boxes for him, on the grounds that anyone saddled with a name like Shane can't be much cop at anything?'

'No, no, Mr Ramsbottom, that is precisely what we must not do. The whole point of scrapping formal exams is that we make a careful appraisal of each separate item for every pupil, and do not let any personal prejudice produce a blanket response. Yes, Dr Grimshaw?'

'This may seem a little pedantic, headmaster, but I did see him push Jane Ellis out of the way in the corridor yesterday. If he is capable of pushing *people*, may we infer he also has the capacity to push *things*? One other point, I did notice him pulling on his gumboots in the cloakroom yesterday lunchtime, but he did need a little help, so I am not sure that qualifies him for the full tick.'

'Headmaster, my view of Shane Abbott is that he pushed off at every opportunity, pulls fast ones, and lifts the dinner money when no one's looking, so can't we just give him his tick and get on to the next item?'

'Now please Mr Jenkins, I hope you and your colleagues in PE are not going to be frivolous about this matter. Before I give a ruling on the technical points raised by Dr Grimshaw, are there any other observations? Ah, Mr Barley.'

'Headmaster, I must protest, we in the English department are totally against this monstrously crude way of dismembering fellow human beings. Shane is a very sensitive boy, and I am not willing to comment in a meeting on his pushing, pulling and lifting ability, except in the strictest confidence and with the full knowledge of his parents.'

'Well, I hope the English staff will revise their position on that. Yes, Mr Battersby, an observation from the maths staff, is it?'

'Only to say that so far as I'm concerned, Shane Abbott is so idle that if he ever summoned up enough energy to lift his pen he'd probably suffer a double hernia.'

'Please, ladies and gentlemen, we must take this seriously. Do understand that by scrapping GCE and CSE and being the first school in Swineshire to go over to pupil profiles we can really put East Swineshire on the map. The business community will be pleased, and the ministers themselves are said to be very interested in what we are doing.'

'Headmaster, we have 180 profiles to complete, each with 200 items. That makes 36,000 "yes" or "no" ticks to be assigned. We have already spent 20 minutes trying to decide on the first item, and at this rate I calculate the exercise will take us 10 years. It is quite clear we cannot agree, so may I make a simple suggestion?'

'Certainly Miss Foley, anything that will get us out of this dreadful impasse and help us decide once and for all about Shane Abbott's pushing, pulling and lifting ability. Please speak out, let us hear it.'

'Couldn't we set an exam?'

11 February 1983

Last words from the rip-off factory

Dear Parent,

Quite a lot has been happening in the school since newsletter 21, so I am writing to bring you up to date. I am delighted to say this will be my last ever parents' newsletter, as I am quitting as head at the end of this term. When I looked at the early retirement deal. I realized that, for doing nothing at all, I would be earning nearly as much as I get now for herniating myself every day.

Indeed, if I took the current school crossing patrol vacancy, I could make up much of the difference by standing outside the school, morning and evening, holding a big lollipop stick. For all the good heads can do nowadays I might as well spend all day standing *inside* the school holding a big lollipop stick. So this will be the last of my mealy-mouthed biennial missives, in which I try to paper over the remorselessly spreading cracks.

The biggest change since my newsletter is the introduction of what is grandly known as local management. This is a joyous misnomer for a system whereby I have to manage the Government's curriculum and the Government's testing programme with a sum of money determined by the Government's formula. In other words it is about as local as the Katmandu Wimpy Bar.

The result of this latest wheeze to give power to the people has been worked out by a formula whose subtlety, I must admit, eludes me. In so far as I can actually understand it, the local authority has to think of a number, add to it the IQ of the chairman of the education committee, (which in our case, I suspect, may reduce the sum), multiply it by some civil servant's hat size and then take away the number you first thought of.

As a result we are some 30,000 smackers worse off and must sharply reduce our expenditure. I have been asked to tell you of the manifold and hare-brained schemes dreamed up by the governors to meet the shortfall. Great hope has been invested in the entrepreneurial powers of your own offspring. If we do live in an area awash with such a rich pool of wealth generating genes, then I am left asking myself why the whole neighbourhood looks like the set from a World War Two film, but that is by the way.

The governors have been convinced by the chairman, whose own chip shop hovers permanently on the brink of oblivion, that we can ape those schools whose pupils are said to be making millions on the side, so we have joined the mini-enterprise scheme. For those whose dustbins are not yet full of child-manufactured junk, let me explain what joining the mini-enterprise scheme will mean in our case.

Your children will in future spend valuable school time manufacturing a succession of substandard, hideously mispainted garden gnomes. Under the mistaken assumption that this will put Britain back on its feet, (and having seen the junk shortly to be launched on an unsuspecting world, I would advise Britain to remain lying peacefully on its back), you will then be expected to feign delight at this manifest garbage, and, no doubt through clenched teeth, actually part with your hard-earned loot to purchase it.

The staff meanwhile are supposed to believe that this rip-off teaches children the meaning of market forces and prepares them for a glittering career in the big world of business, and I suppose to some extent it does. Thus not only will the school make a fortune, it is being argued, but your children will all become millionaires. I have pointed out that, for the second part of this prediction to come true, the great British public would have to consist of millions of people with the critical acumen of an educationally subnormal midge, but my words are ignored.

You may have read about those schools which are levying a £50 voluntary charge on parents to pay a teacher's salary. Our governors are proposing a Rent-a-Teacher scheme instead. For a tenner one of my colleagues will come round to your place and clear a blocked drain, paper over a crack or make a silk purse out of a sow's ear, in other words more or less what they spend the day doing anyway. As you can imagine the National Union of Teachers is delirious about this.

If you wish to take advantage of this scheme, I would advise you to avoid Mr Fosdyke, unless you want the same chaos in your home as we have daily in the school. The pinnacle of his efficiency is to remember to give out the pencils, and successful completion of his attendance register is hailed as a major administrative triumph, the staff are holding a dinner to celebrate.

I am afraid that my own brilliant fund-raising suggestions were dismissed by the governors as the demented ramblings of a demob-happy loon. Thus the coin-op toilet scheme ('10p a pee' was my rather snappy slogan) was not adopted, which is a pity, as we could have had the unique distinction of being the first school in Britain to erase its LMS debt by widdling it away; a fine example to others, I would have thought.

Nor was my suggestion to set up chatlines any more successful. Given that parents have complained for years that they can never discover how their children are getting on, it must be well worth 38p a minute to phone up and find out. Mrs Hardacre, whose classroom voice has always reminded me of the speaking clock, (the content of her lessons has the same level of intellectual power, it should be said), could have told you the time, as her eyes are on the clock most of the day anyway.

Fortunately I have managed to raise a quick hundred myself. I discovered that a local firm was willing to pay £50 a skip for waste paper, so I soon dispatched a couple of skips. It is too early to say yet how the Chief Adviser will react, when he visits us next Tuesday, to the 12 empty shelves in my study which used to house the school's collection of National Curriculum documents, but I will let you know. Suffice it to say that the postman who delivered them all gleefully helped me load up the skips, and I have promised to buy him a new truss out of school funds.

My successor was asked one question at interview, namely, 'What are you like at raising funds?' Personally I would have installed a cash dispenser in the vestibule and saved the salary, but I am proud to be able to hand over the gnome factory in tiptop condition, as I sign off accordingly.

King Gnome

22 June 1990

Hold the Kwality, give us some calibre

The quality season is here again. As the school year unfolds I get more glossy brochures and prospectuses about conferences and consultancies on the theme of 'quality'. For a mere million pounds plus VAT you can attend numerous one-day events entitled The Quality Quality All The Way Seminar, organized by Topp Kwality Seminars plc, Kwality House, Kwality Street, Kwalityville. The only nostalgia I feel nowadays is for the time when Quality Street was a box of chocs.

The problem with the Kwality push is simple. Who could possibly be against it? As with the merits of home-made bread and clean air, who dares dissent? Tempting though it may be to lauch a rival How to Purvey Rubbish Seminar, organized by Naff Seminars plc, Tripe House, Krappville, I cannot see too many takers. The new institutionalized, officially endorsed Kwality is definitely here to stay, the in thing; feel guilty if you demur.

The whole Kwality movement seems to be mesmerized by the precepts of manufacturing. I have often wondered what the significant connection is between making a spigot and running a school or a classroom. There must be one, because the language of Kwality is the language of spigot-making.

If manufacturing spigots of various sizes, you do not want a spigot that is too big or too small for the hole you propose to bung it into. If there is any national petition to ensure that spigots fit the appropriate bung-hole, then put me down as a signatory, as I do feel strongly about it. Spigots must fit holes. But what does the construction of inert lumps of wood and metal have to do with education? Children and teachers are not bungs, honed to fit the appropriate cavity, so no one should pretend they are.

Yet terms like 'calibration' abound. What is there to calibrate? One of the problems with political views of pupil testing is that there is an assumption that the perfect calibration lies just around the corner, if only someone can find it. Go and calibrate your head, Kwality House, if you believe that. All it does is concentrate energy on what is easily calibrated, rather than on what really counts.

I am all in favour of improving education, and indeed of trying to do so in a systematic rather than haphazard way, including quantification where necessary, but not in an overly self-conscious, sculptured, mechanical manner.

You can even get the official team kit nowadays. It is known as BS 5750, a fully calibrated British Standard, which seems to be the official badge of school Kwality. For further oodles, plus VAT, you can go on lots more one-day courses telling you how to win your Kwality tenderfoot badge and woggle.

This leaves just one burning question. If you get the BS 5750 award, do you get a kitemark stamped on your bum?

There are now countless fresh opportunities to learn new acronyms, such as GRASP (Getting Results and Solving Problems). I love these concepts. They open the door to all kinds of entrepreneurial possibilities for the fertile imagination. For only £5,000 plus VAT, we at PRATS (Please Realize All Teachers Skive) can offer you a one-day seminar on a technique for raising money from gullible parents, called TOSH (Tripe Only Suckers, Haha) and reveal our plan for disaffected teachers, under the acronym BILGE (Bored In Lessons? Go Early). Then there is our brilliant solution to school cash-flow problems, known as BALLS (Bugger All Left, Let's Sing).

It is noticeable that real quality does not get drowned in acronyms, nor does it bristle with kitemarks and Kwality labels. 'St Paul's Cathedral, a top quality church'; 'Beethoven, holder of Bonn's official seal of tunefulness'; 'Rembrandt, awarded Dutch Standard 5750 paint mixing kitemark'; 'Shakespeare swears by POEMS (Pen Official English, Mind Spellings)': none of these really have the right ring to them. I can foresee the day when a British Standard teacher is exhibited in the entrance hall to the Department for Education in a glass case under constant temperature and pressure. I bet there are no airholes.

The most pressing need for quality assurance, however, is at the very top of the education system. The conduct of some ministers leaves a lot to be desired.

At his party conference, anxious to please the right wing and show what a tough guy he is, John Patten launched a ferocious attack on Tim Brighouse, chief education officer of Birmingham. I have been chairing the Birmingham Commission, which has been looking into the future of education in that city, so I saw Tim's work at first hand. If ever there was a man of real quality, he must be it.

Every day he goes into a different school. One day in July I left Exeter at five in the morning, spent all day listening to the witnesses who came to give evidence and then sat down in the evening to carry on talking to Tim about Birmingham and its education. The first time I looked at the clock it was half past midnight. I had not felt tired because it was exhilarating to talk to someone with his kind of enthusiasm and commitment. If Tim Brighouse is a madman, then would that the world were full of such engaging nutters.

The problem in a political world sadly bereft of real quality, is that the Government has been in power so long, some of its members think they can fly.

Patten can call parents' representatives 'Neanderthal' for their views, teachers 'Luddites' and Tim Brighouse a 'madman', but he remains fireproof. Nothing he says or does threatens his position, no matter how contemptuous he is of people trying to do their job.

This is the chilling political climate in which we now live. It is high time he was calibrated.

22 October 1993

8

Inside the classroom

If the heads were sometimes the exhausted generals, then classroom teachers were the spirited foot soldiers. Assailed on all sides, attacked by ministers, the press, even school inspectors, they had to get on with the daily job of educating eight million children. Dunkirk humour abounds in school staffrooms, and this chapter records the effects and impact of Government lunacy at classroom level.

Dear Aunt Ada

A recent news report said that policemen were under such stress nowadays, they really needed their own agony column. Why only policemen?

Dear Aunt Ada,
   I am writing to you for advice because I am at my wits' end. You see, I have been teaching in the same primary school for 30 years, and we have just been joined by two new teachers who regard all my methods as old-fashioned and call me a square. As we are only a three-teacher school it is beginning to get me down. Can you help me?
Victoria N. Values

   I know how you and many similar teachers must feel, Victoria, but do not worry. You will be interested to hear that Jane Fonda has produced a new book called The Science of Squareobics. *You sit in a chair in the corner of the staffroom listening to your personal stereo and swinging copies of Beacon Readers in either hand. You will be off the Valium inside six weeks.*

Dear Aunt Ada,
   I was away from school for four days and did not produce a doctor's note because I thought that, under new legislation, you did not require a sick note for less than a week's illness. Now the head tells me that the local authority will be cross. What is my position?
Jean King, Swineshire

   Technically you are quite correct, Jean. The head is confusing the issue with Swineshire's own requirement that teachers give at least three days' notice of their impending or intended death. This is so that the authority has time to think up a good reason why the school should not have a supply teacher, and has nothing to do with sick notes.

Dear Aunt Ada,
   We hear a lot of criticism about sexism or racism in education, but what about ageism? I am a 58-year-old deputy head (pastoral care) and I am fed up of ageist remarks from my younger colleagues like

'Hurry up, grandpa', and 'Have you spent this week's pension yet, Baldy?' What do you suggest I do?'

Silas Q. Gradgrind

You must resist the temptation, Silas, to wear open-necked shirts, medallions, buy a sports car or make any other such silly gestures. Why not ham it up? Try going along the corridors in a bath chair, or, in your pastoral role, wearing a large white toga, carrying a shepherd's crook and calling people 'my son' or 'young miss'. Reply to your colleagues' smart-ass remarks with quips like 'I'm not talking to you until your voice has broken'. The subtle approach is always the best.

Dear Aunt Ada,

I am a drama adviser in a large local authority and for the last 18 months I have been given all the redeployments to deal with. Not only am I fed up with being redeployment officer but I am losing touch with recent developments in drama. I have asked to be relieved of the job but the boss won't hear of it. What can I do?

Lawrence O'Toole

This is an easy one, Lawrence. Since you are the county's official redeployment officer you should redeploy the chief education officer as redeployment officer and make yourself CEO. That way you solve your problem and gain a large increase in salary.

Dear Aunt Ada,

I wonder if you can help me. I work for an objective research institute dedicated to proving that the private sector can knock spots off local authority schools. I know that, given time, I could prove that comprehensive reorganization was responsible for England losing the Ashes, the Estonian earthquake and poor attendances at some First Division matches this season. Unfortunately the Government refuses to fund my research. Can you advise?

Norbert Jekyll-Hyde
Centre for Pathetic Studies

I know how you feel, Norbert, when everybody and everything seem to be against you. I am sending you eight sure-fire draws for next Saturday's pools coupon and the address of the Distressed Gentlemen's Assistance Society who may be able to assist.

Dear Aunt Ada,

I am writing to you, esteemed person, in great desperation. I am president of large Japanese robotics company. My company makes most advanced robots in whole world. We were given top secret assignment to produce robots to wreck Russian economy. Two of our most brilliant robots, destined for Moscow, have been lost. The first one is sixth generation model designed to ruin Soviet economy in guise of Education Minister. It is codenamed KJ6 and is programmed to produce hundreds of bizarre ideas bringing whole country to total exhaustion. The second, programmed to be junior minister and to bore Russians to oblivion, has Japanese codename No-Fun-Dunn (translation: death by a thousand yawns). Unfortunately KJ6 has no manual over-ride, and its eyes will suddenly bulge and it may detonate. Our sales manager believes both models may have been sent to London by mistake. Can you help?

B. Yamahatsu, president
Wishiwashi Corporation, Tokyo

The DES tells me, Mr Yamahatsu, that another of your robots, Boi-son has been successfully dismantled, but they have no knowledge of the two you mention.

18 November 1983

Under fire in the classroom

'Your radio is jammed . . . you're pinned down by enemy fire . . . two of your men are badly wounded . . .' No, this is not a task on a management course for heads preparing to implement the national curriculum. You may recognize it as the text of a press advert for army officer recruitment designed especially to attract arts graduates.

The ad shows the above captions alongside three photographs of soldiers on the battlefield, and underneath the third of these, which depicts a man lying on a stretcher swathed in bandages, is the banner headline, 'What use is a degree in medieval history?' It seems to have escaped the wizards who conceived the ad that an army officer who does indeed possess a degree in medieval history, and who finds one of his men with a wounded leg, would probably saw it off and pour a bottle of whisky over it.

All of this set me thinking along two lines. The first was that this could be the style of the new Department of Education and Science recruiting literature for El Cheapo licensed teachers. There could be photographs of children sitting on the chest of some hapless untrained licensed teacher, hiding the chalk, pinning him against the wall or throwing paper aeroplanes at him, and the text could read: 'Your mind is blank . . . two children are sitting on your chest . . . your classroom is on fire . . .', followed by the banner headline, 'What use is your diploma in basket-weaving now, smarty pants?'

The second strand of thought was a much more serious one about the notion of 'relevance' in education. The answer given by the copywriter of the army officer ad to his own question about the utility of a degree in medieval history reads: 'A lot of use. You have a trained mind. The capacity to absorb information rapidly and to act on it. It could save the lives of your men. That is why we value graduates of any discipline.' In other words, the assumption is that skills acquired in one domain are transferable to another.

This raises several issues about the purpose and style of education, whether in the context of the Technical and Vocational Education Initiative or the National Curriculum. It is interesting that major employers, like the armed forces, are going out of their way to hire people who appear, on the surface, to have had little 'relevant' preparation.

There are aspects of human learning where it does make sense to learn in sequence a set of 'relevant' skills and then combine them into an organic whole. Certain sports require very specific skills like passing or running with the ball, and practising these singly and together is 'relevant' training. On the other hand, in a game like snooker there is no real point in practising separately the art of walking round the table, even though snooker involves a lot of it, because anyone not actually on a life support machine can do it already.

We learned to walk because we were motivated to do so, and we learned it in a form which is generally useful by walking whenever it made sense or there was a need. If someone had tried to put one of our feet in front of the other at an early age as a detached part of a self-conscious, 'relevant' structured skills package, we would probably have nose-dived more often than we did.

This highlights one worry I have about the implementation of the National Curriculum, especially in primary schools. Some people seem to be under the impression, because guidelines and attainment targets are expressed as discrete pieces of behaviour, that these are topics which must be taught in sequence and ticked when completed.

This rigid notion of teaching, which is, thank goodness, being discouraged by the National Curriculum Council, would go against what we know about how young children learn. Sometimes they do learn directly by tackling a topic or skill head on, but equally often they learn in a more oblique way.

Most of us have learned to smile not because we successfully completed a single 'relevant' course on smiling but rather as a result of several inter-related experiences. The challenge to teachers is to judge, for each requirement of the National Curriculum, whether it makes sense to cover it separately, or organically, or both.

Enough of the boring stuff. Let me finish by telling you about a Puffin book for young children I have just read, entitled. I tease you not, *Master Bun the Baker's Boy*. It tells of Master Bun who is browned off with his present job and desperately wants to be a butcher's boy (Home Secretary?), dreams about being a bank robber's boy (Chancellor of the Exchequer?), and finally becomes a conjuror's boy (Prime Minister?). I loved it, especially when Mr Creep's dog ran off with his sausages.

24 March 1989

I'm gonna wash that man right out . . .

The news that it might be possible to sue someone for stress came as a bit of a surprise. Like most people, I had always assumed that stress was something one simply had to put up with in a rapidly moving society.

It is, apparently, permissible to take action for 'traumatic stress', if some horrendous event takes place, and it might even be possible to sue for 'cumulative stress', if there is a build-up over time.

So let us start by suing the Government. 'I submit, m'lud, that my client suffered from cumulative stress between the years 1988 and 1993, when he was sent 3,427 official documents, most of which contradicted each other, and from traumatic stress on the morning of November 10 1993, when he unexpectedly received not a single official document and spent the rest of the week in the intensive care unit worrying about what had gone wrong.'

Stress-related illness is estimated to cost several billion pounds a year. Little or no stress counselling is available in this country, though in the United States it is recognized that teacher burn-out and other manifestations of tension can cost thousands, so some schools have a budget to pay for professional help for those who may need it.

There is widespread ignorance of the aetiology of stress in Britain, and those who suffer are often thought to be wimps or skivers with a vivid imagination.

According to the textbooks, stress can be brought about by anxiety, which in turn is caused by such factors as overwork, bad personal relationships, conditions of employment (or lack of it), uncertainty about the present and future, and especially by aggravation over which the victim has no control. However, there is more to it than that.

One of the most severe forms of tension is what we doctors call 'prat-related stress'. This occurs when one particular Wally lies at the heart of the aggravation. The stress comes about because it is actually the Wally, not the sufferer, who has the problem.

Take the case of some overbearing, authoritarian swine, who has himself never had a spark of imagination and creativity. The creative person becomes the victim, as any ideas put forward are ritually rubbished, and so feels a failure and becomes stressed. The real patient, however, should be the Wally, who can only cope by victimizing others.

Nowadays another common manifestation is 'paper-related stress'. The sufferer sees spots before the eyes, becomes dizzy and, in extreme cases, actually vomits over any piece of A4 paper, ring-bound folder or document marked 'Department for Education'.

The official medical treatment is for the patient to while away the hours reading and re-reading the Government's ludicrous and now obsolete *Anthology of Great Key Stage 3 English Literature*, alongside which every other printed document seems reasonable.

The behaviourist cure is for the patient first to be given photographs of a filing cabinet to look at. When no longer nauseous, single sheets of A4 may be handled gently, until the victim can actually hold, without trembling, a whole National Curriculum folder. Only at the later stages of therapy may a SAT be fondled. Patients are not sent home until they can fill in a checklist without perspiring profusely or resorting to profane language. Few make it thus far, so most are still inside.

It is one thing to be stressed, quite another to be cured, and it is in the field of physics that much about stress is explained. Hooke's Law states that when you stretch a spring, the tension in it is proportional to the length it is extended. In other words, the longer you pull it, the more the stress.

Eventually it twangs itself to death and becomes the sad, discarded piece of useless metal we all have lying around our wastepaper baskets. Brilliant. Good old Hooke. If you are at the end of your tether and someone gives you a hard time, just say, 'Boing, boing – phut'. It beats the traditional two-word response.

The hardest solution for many teachers is to step back and put everything in perspective. Despite assertions to the contrary from politicians and press, most teachers are conscientious and get terribly upset if they cannot meet their own aspirations.

Few therefore, are able to adopt the highly successful 'Soddit solution', devised by Dr Soddit, a nineteenth-century physician, whereby the victim pronounces his name like a mantra, muttering 'Soddit, Soddit', over and over again.

The temptation is to find a scapegoat who can be blamed for everything. Just as children affix their anxieties to bogeymen or giants, so they can focus uncertainties and stresses on something specific, adults need a hate figure to shoulder responsibility for all that oppresses them. Sometimes a comical shape will appear conveniently like a pantomime demon, popping up through a trap-door in the stage, begging to be scapegoated. Such is the fate of John Patten, handcrafted to fill the role.

Yet old Wash and Go is merely the current totemic symbol of a deep underlying malaise. The Secretary of State has accrued immense powers – more than 500 of them within five years. As Edward Heath pointed out during the second reading of the 1988 Education Bill, Patten's predecessors took more powers than any other cabinet minister. It is now an awesome, and indeed awful, example of the madness of long-distance, central control.

There would be stresses in teaching anyway, because it is a demanding job. But they have increased because nowadays one individual, sitting miles away from the realities of his policies, is empowered by the state to do virtually what he likes, irrespective of the effects on or responses of teachers and parents. Small wonder that the rhythmic noise coming from many schools is 'Boing, boing, boing, phut – Soddit'.

19 November 1993

Answer the questionnaire, it's pay-risible

Wanting to be sure about Government education policy before the year was laid to rest, I thought it was worth a nanosecond or two trying to complete the Department for Education 1993 Big SAT for Teachers. In case you never saw your copy, here it is. It will probably be used next year as the basis for performance-related pay rises (i.e. there won't be any).

1 The 1993 Education Act made opting out:
(a) interesting – you get shot of the LEA.
(b) attractive – you get shot of financial problems.
(c) compulsory – you get shot if you don't.

2 The last Government White Paper was called:
(a) Choice and Diversity.
(b) Chance and Adversity.
(c) This is Crap Even By Our Standards.

3 The Dearing Committee:
(a) made the National Curriculum simpler.
(b) is trying to make the National Curriculum simpler.
(c) is still only part way through reading the National Curriculum and hopes to report by late 1997.

4 The new rules for sex education are:
(a) it is compulsory, but parents can withdraw their children.
(b) education is OK, but sex isn't.
(c) teachers must wear a condom on their head when teaching it.

5 1994's truancy figures will be:
   (a) used to calculate head teachers' salaries.
   (b) assembled by Walter Mitty.
   (c) much lower than the 1993 truancy figures, though the true
       story will be anybody's guess.

6 The Government's policy on training, insofar as anyone can
   actually work it out, is:
   (a) anyone can teach who has either a BEd, or a degree plus a
       PGCE.
   (b) anyone can teach who is not actually on a life support
       machine.
   (c) anyone can teach.

7 OFSTED stands for:
   (a) Office for Standards in Education.
   (b) Off For Some Trip in Educational Dreamland.
   (c) Often Far Sillier Than Education Deserves.

8 The role of the lay inspector is:
   (a) to give an intelligent lay person's view.
   (b) to confirm that if anyone can teach, then anyone can
       inspect teaching.
   (c) to look bewildered, contribute bugger all, but still collect
       200 quid a day.

9 The biggest health hazard facing head teachers when completing Government league table information sheets is to:
   (a) get writer's cramp.
   (b) get Pinocchio's nose.
   (c) die laughing.

10 The Government's greatest contribution to raising standards in
   1993 was:
   (a) introducing the starred grade A at A level.
   (b) making every school fly the Union Jack.
   (c) merging NCC and SEAC to make SCARPER-
       WHILEYOUCAN.

11 The Government's chief hope for 1994 is that it should be:
   (a) even better than good old scintillating 1993.
   (b) 365 days of unadulterated mirth.
   (c) just like 1894.

12 In keeping with the recent tradition of appointing an even bigger comedian as Minister than the previous incumbent, John Patten's successor will be:

(a) Bob Hope.

(b) Laurel and Hardy.

(c) impossible to find.

If you answered mainly (a) then you may qualify for the .001 per cent performance-related pay bonus of 15 pence proposed by John Major, the man who said he wanted every teacher to be able to afford a decent car.

If you answered mainly (b) then your sense of humour will allow you to survive 1994.

If you answered mainly (c) then you are a serious subversive, who probably does dangerously foolish things, like working in education.

Happy New Year, friend.

31 December 1993

Don't mention secondments, Basil

Dad, what's a secondment? Younger teachers could be forgiven for not knowing a term that was in common use until the mid-1980s. Back in the early 1970s, the James Report had recommended that teachers should have one term of release every seven years. That would have meant the equivalent of two years or so over a professional lifetime.

Teachers might have expected, therefore, to have a year's secondment for some significant retraining or for taking a higher degree, a one-term release on another occasion, and lots of shorter opportunities for professional refreshment.

Instead there followed a period of unparalleled change in education, during which teachers took on board the national curriculum, standard assessment tasks, local management, the GCSE, the Technical and Vocational Initiative, and a host of other 'reforms', with an occasional one-day or two-day conference to support them.

Primary teachers are buried under a welter of subject knowledge demands, with virtually no chance to get out of school and clue themselves up about the Aztecs, electricity and magnetism, micro-computers, or the aerodynamics of the somersault. Small wonder that so many teachers appear on *Mastermind* and *Brain of Britain*. It is amazing what you can mug up if you are used to reading about the history of plough design at six in the morning.

In the mid 1980s, more than 2,000 teachers used to be seconded to universities. Nowadays, in these changed times, full-time higher degree students consist of a tiny cluster of trainees for educational psychology qualifications, a minute collection of pools winners financing themselves, and a small, heroic band of teachers who also pay their own way but go bankrupt in the process. Most higher qualifications are obtained on a part-time basis, by teachers studying early in the morning or late at night when they are knackered. It is not the best way to study at the highest level.

As the Government applies more commercial and financial screws to schools, I half expected they might set up a central pool for teachers whose schools cannot afford to release them (like all 25,000 primary and secondary schools), but that would reek too much of socialism. Not even support for the odd MEd in roof repairing, the occasional MPhil in box-ticking or PhD in recycling used paper has been forthcoming.

The development of school-based in-service courses is one of the few real gains to emerge from this bleak period. Many schools have put in place impressive staff development programmes on slender resources. The frustrating feature of short one and two-day events, however, is that they often end just when people's appetites have been whetted.

What is also fascinating is the development, alongside school-based in-service training, of a significant hotel-based INSET culture. 'We've got a video recorder,' one hotel manager told me proudly when I asked about facilities for conferences. You could see how he was thinking: 'Other punters want to stare blankly at horse racing, but teachers like watching boring old videos on primary science.' Sadly, the video recorder was as knackered as many of the teachers attending weekend conferences.

Listen to any conversation about conferences in hotels. 'We're going to have our next staff conference at the Fawlty Towers Conference Centre,' the head announces proudly. Does anyone want to know the theme of this vital professional exchange? Certainly not. Let's get the important questions settled first: 'What's the food like?' 'Have they got satellite?' 'Is there a bar?' 'Have they got a jacuzzi?'. To hell with: 'Can we have a session on competitive tendering?'

Another hotel manager clearly appreciated the realities of cash-strapped schools when he told me, with no hint of irony: 'We do special cut-price deals for teachers including low-cost food.' I know what he meant, but it just sounded as if you had to kip in the bike shed, and would be served hard peas and sago pudding for dinner, with someone patrolling up and down to put you in detention if you flicked peas at the guests.

In fact, hotels will probably take over the whole of education before long. You can already get your full OFSTED inspector's badge after a week in a hotel. Stay two weeks and you can practise as a brain surgeon. Basil Fawlty has become a minister. For schools in dire financial straits it is also a great consolation to have a conference in one hotel chain that went £1 billion in the red last year. It puts things into perspective.

Lots of other official conferences organized by Government agencies now take place in hotels, all part of the private enterprise culture. They are often expensive, but the food is good. The Department for Education has just approved the official menu for all its conferences this year:

> *Lame duck soup, or Patten de foie gras*
> *Plaice to avoid*
> *Coq-up au vin, or Complete turkey*
> *Raspberry fool*
> *(In-service not included, VAT a fiasco)*

8 April 1994

Nasty noises under the curriculum bonnet

It was a serious suggestion. I was looking through an American journal the other day in which it was proposed that teachers should be re-licensed from time to time. The argument was that teaching was a profession in which you could easily become clapped out, so every year or two you needed to be tested to see if you were still roadworthy.

I had never really thought of an MOT for teachers, but I must say that if the purpose of such tests is to get rid of old bangers that have been around for the past 15 years or so, then members of the Government must be a prime target.

The thought of an annual MOT test applied to ministers has a certain appeal to it, especially if it consigned a few old wrecks to the knacker's yard. Baker would have received the thumbs down on oil pressure and lubrication (too much grease), Patten would have got a cross against every single category on the test report, and Clarke would have failed just for being the complete meathead that he was.

I felt that Baker's and Patten's tachometers were severely defective and needed recalibrating. They always gave false readings. Baker's multi-million pound publicity binge started it by pretending that everything was going better and faster than it really was. Patten's tachometer must have been manufactured on Jupiter, because it certainly doesn't register what is happening on this planet.

Apparently parents are Neanderthal (surely that should read 'right at the centre of our policies'), national tests have been fully accepted (er, does he mean 'boycotted') and the opting-out policy is incredibly popular, the jewel in the crown (come again, did he say 96 per cent of schools haven't actually done it?). More money than ever is being put into schools (did I hear the words 'teacher redundancies'?) and higher education is booming (so all those A-level candidates who won't get in this year because of Clarke's budget cuts, and universities being fined if they go over quota, are a figment of someone's imagination?).

Most of these ministers would also fail on steering. There has been a distinct pull to the right in recent years, causing the whole educational enterprise to veer out of control and crash into oncoming curriculum directives. There is a lot of wear and slack here. You can try to turn them without having any effect on their direction, a bit like unguided missiles.

Perhaps ministers should be labelled like the cars offered in newspaper small ads, though it would be the one occasion when 'full service record' would actually be a disadvantage. Phrases such as 'Looks good, but no MOT', 'right wing damage' or 'would consider exchange for better model, cash adjustment as appropriate', ought to be made available under the Citizen's Charter. The last of these is an attractive possibility, though it would presumably take a huge cash adjustment to get a Jaguar for an underpowered Reliant Robin.

So if the Government did set up an annual MOT for teachers, what would it look like? It would probably be administered by a back-street quango, involve ticking hundreds of boxes in triplicate, and be ideologically loaded. I hesitate to speculate on the test criteria, knowing that the Government is always in the market for barmy ideas, but their very own MOT for teachers would no doubt look something like this:

Braking
Should pull to the right.
Must stop dead anything that looks like moving us out of the 19th century.
Holds firm when sliding down the slippery slope into Excrement Creek.

Steering
No wobble when implementing Government policy, however daft.
Steers straight over the top of anything that looks imaginative.

Lights
Never teaches in an enlightened or illuminating manner.
Teaching must dip, and never dazzle.

Tyres
Well shod (flat brogues, or at least 1 mm of sole left on Hush Puppies).

Indicators
Blinks 40 to 50 times a minute when vital bits held in vice by Government.
Never flashes during sex education lessons.

Lubrication
Can hold a full eight pints after school.
Keeps education running smoothly whenever the Government screws it up.

Battery
Fully charged, even when used all day and half the night.
Positive about SATs, negative about boycotts.

Acceleration
Pulls away smoothly when asked to join a union.
Happy to move slowly up the salary scale.

Transmission
Stands at the front of the class spouting facts that no-one understands.
Reverses easily when sent a totally different National Curriculum document.

Bodywork
Well used to, and so never complains about, peeling paint.
Cracks skilfully covered up.

Windscreen
Transparent and gullible.
Covered in droppings from on high.

3 June 1994

All you would never want for Christmas

There are plenty of charity Christmas gift catalogues this year. All the proceeds from this one will go to the Kenneth Baker Home for Terminally Bewildered Teachers.

Festive presents . . .

For her: *OFSTED Home Inspection Kit.* Inspect your own school with this official Office for Standards in Education kit. Numerous absolutely pointless checklists enable you to compute whether you have more or fewer felt-tipped pens than the national average, and whether your board dusters are 'generally satisfactory'.

Price £5,000 (£30,000 for large-school version). Life-size inflatable lay inspector with fixed gormless smile, £2 extra. Off Rip Products Plc. ('Anyone can do it.' Arthur Dewhurst, Butcher.)

For him: *Ron's Firefighting Pack.* Deal with any emergency with the Ron Dearing Firefighting Pack. Includes flameproof suit, fire extinguisher, axe and bucket of water. Just the thing for dealing with difficult governors, awkward parents and the many complete prats you meet in education nowadays.

Price £8.99, SCAA Enterprises. ('It soon put me out,' J. Patten.)

For the kids: *Bendi-Flexi Minister Doll.* Talking doll with red nose and revolving bow-tie. Press button and voice says, 'Standards of GCSE are going down, so I'll ask HMI to report on the matter', or 'Standards of GCSE are going up, so I hereby claim credit for our league table policy'. Hours of fun as the kids show it to their teachers and give them a nervous breakdown as they try to make sense of it all.

Price £29.99, Bullshit Bendi Toys Inc.

Spoof Inspection Letter. Realistic letter on official-looking OFSTED stationery. It states:

'Dear . . . OFSTED will be bringing a team of 12 inspectors to inspect your school on . . .'

All the kids have to do is type in the name of their headteacher and school, and a date about two days ahead. Then they just sit back and watch the head rush off to the staff toilets in a panic. £1.99 Sado-Maso Stationery. ('Laugh? I nearly widdled myself,' K. Clarke.)

Books and games

The Good Excuse Guide. This comprehensive guide brings together some of the best apologies for a lousy position in your local exams league table. Contains classics such as, 'We was robbed', 'It was a year of two halves, Brian', and 'Come next year's league tables we'll be there or thereabouts', as well as novelties such as 'The caretaker was off that week' and, 'Yes, but if you use statistical adjustment to partial out the effects of social class, we actually came top'.
Price £11.99, Whinge Books.

English-Bakerspeak Bilingual Dictionary. Two-volume dictionary with thousands of entries, both Bakerspeak–English and English–Bakerspeak. Contains all the essential terms, including 'deliver the curriculum', 'fulfil attainment targets' and 'scrymzzxx your breeglebums'. £99.99, British Bakerspeak Society. ('Mr Baker makes exceedingly good marshmallow,' Mr Kipling.)

Opt-out: Exciting board game for several players. Throw dice to see who opts out. Successful player gets best chair, a box of chocolates and a free meal, while other players have to sit on the floor and eat broken glass. It's unfair, but it's a hell of a laugh. £25,000,000 (and that's just for technology projects). Grant-Maintained Gizmos Unlimited.

Christmas entertainment

Carry on Testing (At a multiplex cinema/school all too near you). Pure British traditional (nowadays) farce with all the usual 'Carry on' team. Kenneth Williams as Colonel Fruitcake, Hattie Jacques as Felicity Rotating-Eyeballs, and Sid James as Harry Fastbuck are put in charge of educational testing with hilarious results. Kenneth Williams sets the papers, Hattie Jacques translates them into Old Norse and Sid James tries to sell them to a gullible American tourist. Teachers' boycott ensues. Pure escapist fantasy; it could never happen in real life.

Last Quango in Paris (Boxing Day, Eurosport). Tells how a desperate Government, having stitched up every public body in Britain, has to go abroad to set up new quangos.

Your questions answered

I recently found a line from Keats as the motto in a Christmas cracker. Does this demonstrate that Government policies are working and we are becoming a more literate nation? No. It demonstrates what happened to those Government *Anthologies of Great English Literature*, gleefully shredded by English teachers after their boycott of key stage 3 testing.

We haven't got much money in our school, so is it worth buying a few National Lottery tickets before Christmas?

The odds against winning the top prize in the National Lottery are about 14 million to one. The likelihood of the Government giving you any more money is about a million billion to one. Go and buy the tickets now.

Are there many turkeys about this Christmas? Yes, but they're not ministers any more.

9 December 1994

9

County Hall

Local authorities, remember them? At the start of the 1980s they were quite powerful, and I spent a great deal of time satirizing pompous councillors who misused their power. By the 1990s they had been written off by a Government hoping that, if most schools opted out, and with schools having more direct control over their finances, they would fade quietly and bloodlessly away. The best tried to find a new role, while some merely wrung their hands and floundered in dismay around the fringes of their local league tables.

Words in edgeways

'Hello? Ah, Parkinson here, Chief Adviser for in-service. Look, sorry to 'phone you so late, but I don't seem to be sleeping too well these days, and it was on my mind to give you a ring about next Tuesday's conference.'

'Just a minute, I'm not at my best at 11.30. That's the day conference for your county heads on "Making the best of falling rolls with almost no resources" isn't it?'

'Well, that was what they originally asked for, but we've rejigged it a bit, and the theme is now "Into the eighties – an exciting decade of challenge". The CEO didn't want another of those awful public griping sessions'.

'So you don't want me to give the opening address.'

'Oh no, quite the contrary. It's very good of you to come such a long way to talk at our conferences, and we value enormously an outsider's contribution, particularly from someone like yourself based in a university and able to speak his mind. I mean feel free to say anything you like, but I thought I'd just put you in the picture about one or two things locally. Will you be saying anything about education for leisure, I know it's one of your themes?'

'Well, yes, I'd probably mention it *en passant* so to speak?'

'I wonder if you could soft pedal it a bit. We've had a spot of bother with the unions on that one, you know bans on out-of-school activities, that sort of thing. Fire the starting gun in the egg-and-spoon race once a year and they expect a scale 4 some of them. And if you could keep off caretakers while you're on the subject.'

'Caretakers? I hadn't really. . .'

'Well, of course, you couldn't know because you don't see our local press, but after your opening address at last year's conference . . .'

'The one on "Running a school with almost no resources" wasn't it?'

'Again that was the original title the heads wanted, but if you remember we eventually called it "Creative curriculum planning". Anyway that's by the way. Well old Babbage, he's a head in the north of the county, retired last Christmas and obviously demob happy at the time, said in the plenary session that he would love to have a full education for leisure programme in his school if only Adolf Hitler would deign to unlock the building. Unfortunately, the county hall caretaker was sweeping up backstage at the time, quick phone call to NUPE, and bob's your uncle, a fortnight's strike.'

'I'm sorry, I never knew...'

'Oh it's not your fault. Will you say anything about music, do you think?'

'Didn't I touch on it last year? I think I talked about raising expectations in the arts or something.'

'What you actually said was that you'd heard that the music in the county was pathetic. It gave my colleague Swanson, the music adviser, a triple coronary I can tell you. What you couldn't realize at the time is that Swanson, who incidentally teeters permanently on the edge of a nervous breakdown, was in any case in the CEO's bad books for buying a job lot of 300 bassoons from some bankrupt stock he'd come across. Needless to say, nobody plays them, and I know one head has plants growing in a couple in his study. Incidentally, are you planning to say anything about the advisory service in general, because we're a bit fragile at the moment?'

'I suppose it's possible. I didn't really cover it last year.'

'Well, not directly, but when, if you remember, you talked about creative planning being choked by "armies of pen-pushing parasites and over-fed bureaucrats", you probably didn't notice friend Babbage doubled up with mirth. Sure enough, as soon as the lecture was over, the snide little toad oiled over to me chortling "rumbled again" before waddling off to the bar with his cronies. It can take up to half an hour nowadays to pick the knives out of your back after one of these bunfights.'

'I hadn't realized. I'm awfully sorry. I mean is there anything I shouldn't...'

'Goodness me, don't worry yourself about it. You say anything you like, don't let me put you off. No it's just local politics. I suppose you chaps in universities are above this sort of thing. Are you expecting to put in a word, by the way, about teachers' centres?'

'Well, I haven't really...'

'Only it was all a bit ironical. You remember last year you got a round of applause when you said you saw an important age dawning for teachers' centres, and that the wardens would be very close to the "leisure and the future" debate? Well ours are going to have unlimited leisure in the future because we're closing all the centres.'

'Gosh, I'm sorry, I just never thought. I mean is there...'

'Conditions of service and Burnham, I should keep off that one. Lunchtime supervision is not the CEO's favourite topic at the moment, since one of our heads is suing the authority over having to do it all on his own. Got his head stuck in some railings spying on illicit smokers, or gamblers or something.'

'I hadn't intended . . .'

'Steer clear of school closures perhaps. Parents in the classroom might be tricky.'

'Do you think . . .'

'Governors, don't mention them. Put on courses for them and the creeps repay you by asking very nasty questions at governors' meetings. In-service could be a beggar, cover for absent teachers, that sort of thing. But look, I mean, I only rang you to say we're all looking forward to next Tuesday, and you feel free to say whatever you like.'

28 November 1980

Department of Redeployment

'Hello, is that East Swineshire Comprehensive School? It's Tom Jackson here, Chief Adviser, can you put me through to the headmaster please? . . . Ah, Brian, it's Tom here. Sorry to bother you, but I just wanted a word about those two maths posts you've been advertising.'

'Oh hello Tom. Yes, we're all really excited about it. It's the first time we've been able to make a couple of new appointments for ages, and you know how much we need fresh young blood here: average age 93, cloakroom full of bath chairs, spending half our capitation on Phyllosan, that sort of thing.'

'So what sort of people are you looking for?'

'Just young ones, preferably a couple straight out of training. I'll be honest with you Tom, to get a bit of youth on the premises I'd take on a couple of boy scouts or girl guides. I'm pig sick of being called "Young Brian" by the rest of the staff. I suppose I ought to be flattered but at 48 it tells you something about the age structure here. The maths people would prefer someone who's a dab hand at snooker and darts as well as being under 50, and the head of science has just sent me a note about their department meeting where it was democrat-ically decided to settle for anyone with big knockers.'

'But what about the recent HMI report that said some probationers were not all that good?'

'That report was rubbish. Hardly surprising the poor things couldn't teach straight, with a government heavy watching in the back row. Anyway the HMIs are even older than us. Ours has difficulty staying awake, and we have to get the kids to show him out because he always forgets where his car is. No Tom, we've got to have a couple of youngsters, it's like a morgue in here. No wonder they built the new crematorium across the road, half the bloody customers are sitting in our staffroom waiting to have coronaries if they're asked to stay for a parents' evening. I've seen more life in a geriatric ward.'

'Look Brian, I'll be absolutely frank with you. As you know we in in this authority have a redeployment problem . . .'

'I was about to say "over my dead body", but as one of the few people here not on a life support machine that would be in bad taste. I'm not having any redeployed teachers Tom, and that's final. The last thing you want in an intensive care unit is more patients.'

'Now be fair Brian, we've got some absolutely cracking teachers available for redeployment, and I can't understand why you heads are so neurotic about it.'

'What about Simkins? We took him off your hands to help the authority and look what happened. You told me he would be useful on our health education programme, but I assumed you meant as a teacher not as a specimen.'

'I was told he had given up drinking.'

'Well he had, but at the Christmas party he broke into the stock-cupboard and downed half of next term's Phyllosan. He's paralytic most days, and we use him as a visual aid to show the kids the evil ravaging effects of alcohol on the human body.'

'We've got this really good chap Brian. I'm not having you on, he's done a smashing job at North Swineshire.'

'How old is he?'

'He's 63, but honestly Brian he's a really young 63. Look, it's all very well you cracking up laughing, but I've got a hell of a job here. The chief was all for just sending you a couple of people, no choice, but the county solicitor advised that under the Unsolicited Goods Act if we didn't collect them within three months you'd be legally entitled to mail them back postage unpaid, or, worse, dispose of them.'

'I don't know whether you've heard Tom, but our Swineshire Heads Association has started a new consumer magazine like *Motoring Which?* and *Holiday Which?* called *Redeployment Which?* so I know all about this month's best buys, and there are no maths teachers in that category. In fact all the maths teachers on offer failed the British Standards Safety test or something as far as I recall and I don't fancy taking on the pedagogical equivalent of leaking valves and Hong Kong wiring.'

'Look Brian, let's see if we can do a deal. You can have one brand new teacher, if you'll take a redeployment for the other post, could that be fairer? Now this could suit you down to the ground. You know how the authority has been slow-timing your request for a new science block, well we've got this arsonist . . .'

22 October 1982

Local authorities

Right, listen Level Nine. I've told you before, if you want a national curriculum grade 15 for this module on 'One Hundred Years of Private Education, 1988–2088' you're going to have to pay attention, otherwise I'll get the chief executive to reschedule you for home study. Then you can find out for yourself just how easy it is to get off grade 14 with only your video-modem to help you.

Now today we'll be looking at the role of local authorities prior to the full privatization of education in 2008. What do you mean, you don't know what local authorities are, Fotheringay? Did you not access the late twentieth and early twenty-first century social structures video, like I asked you to? I sometimes wonder why I bother. If teacher strikes weren't a capital offence I'd withdraw my labour some days, I can tell you.

Well, for the benefit of Fotheringay and anyone else whose work station was on the blink last night, let me recap events for you. Back in 1988 the country was divided up into 104 administrative zones so far as education was concerned. Each of these was called a local education authority, or LEA for short.

When, in the early 1990s, schools were given their first push into privatization by taking responsibility, at local level, for finances, hiring and firing of teachers and various other matters which are taken for granted nowadays, some LEAs began to dissolve. It started simply enough with the dismissal of staff after the 1995 Charities Act, which offered a bounty of a new building and up to half a million pounds in cash, that's about five million Euromarks in today's currency, to any school opting out of its local authority. This bounty system had already been operating informally since about 1990, but making it official immediately encouraged half the schools in the country to leave local authority control.

The outcome of all this was that the LEAs were left with very few staff and their only function was to support a small number of schools, mainly in poorer areas. As their revenue from the Government decreased, their problem increased. In the end it seemed kindest simply to abolish them, and this is what happened some years later when Education Minister, Sir Oliver Letwin, took his 2008 Education Privatization Act through the House of Thatcher, which had replaced Parliament two years earlier.

Even though this Act was originally known as 'Olly's Folly' there was little resistance to it because education was, by then, the only unprivatized service. Some LEAs tried desperately to put on a few courses for teachers and chief executives to ensure survival, but most preferred to attend courses at newly privatized polyversities and teachers' centres, so that particular hope for survival soon dried up.

Now what I'd like you to do before next Thatcherday's lesson is to write a comparison between last year's 2088 Education Act and what we've just been talking about. The exact title is 'Give a historical critique of the more controversial aspects of the 2088 Education Deprivatization Act', so let's just discuss it before you leave. Any suggestions?

Yes, Peterson, I think it would be fair to say that the present Government feels nostalgia for the twentieth century and has made the issue of Elizabethan values a central plank of its reform programme. Indeed, you may find that its plans to group clusters of private schools together under 100 regional councils to improve efficiency, and then finance them with Government-provided and locally-raised money, has some similarities with what we have just been talking about.

Quite right, Sanders, it should be more effective to offer services to schools from a regional centre instead of each school providing its own at a high unit cost. And yes, we shall have to wait and see, but you may also be right in guessing that each school will, in future, no longer need to employ its own part-time educational psychologist, its 10 professional fundraisers, its 11 part-time national curriculum advisers, its four senior and six junior accountants and its two lawyers.

What's that, Fotheringay? While we're at it we could what? Put all the schools in London together, yes, go on boy, it looks promising, and set up a new single regional authority for the whole city, yes, go on, this sounds brilliant, and call it, what did you say? Go on boy, speak up, the Inner London what?

23 February 1990

New liberties made simple

For those who are still confused about local management of schools, even after the past six weeks of pull-out supplements in *The TES*, here is the final definitive version of all the essential terms and concepts.

Q: I am still unsure what LMS actually stands for. One of my colleagues insists it is a now defunct railway company, but others tell me it has something do with schools. Can you clear it up once and for all?

A: *Linguistics experts are divided about the origin of the term. One head thought it meant Let's Move South, so he retired to the Costa del Sol. Current opinion favours one of three explanations: Lend Me Sixpence, Lots More Suffering and Left Me Speechless.*

Q: I do not really understand how teachers' salaries work nowadays, though I think they are fixed by a body called the IAC. Is it true that governors will be responsible for handing out bonus payments for teachers under LMS, and can you explain the rather complicated set of what I think are called Insensitive Allowances?

A: *You are quite right. Since the abolition of the Burnham Committee the Government has set up a body to determine teachers' salaries, known as the IAC, which stands for It's A Carve-up. There are five extra allowances for teachers which governors can distribute for different purposes. Allowance A is for Apathy when you can't think what else to do. B stands for Bribery, because it is often used to keep good young teachers who threaten to move elsewhere. C is for Come on Sunshine, as this is the reply from teachers who feel they are worth a great deal more. Allowance D stands for Desperate, because it is frequently the only way of recruiting or retaining someone in the shortage area, and E equals Every Blue Moon. There are rumours that the Government may extend the scheme with three additional grades – F for Forget it, G for Greasers and H for Ha Bloody Ha.*

Q: The LMS supplement which dealt with salaries for senior staff like heads and deputies said that, from January 1991, there will be 49 points on the senior staff salary scales, and that a head or deputy can move up at the discretion of the local authority or governing body in the light of national criteria covering responsibilities, the school's catchment area and his or her performance. How will this work?

A: *There was in fact a misprint in this particular supplement. Instead of 49 points, it should have read 49 pints. The criteria determine how many pints the head or deputy should be given. Those who are already walking somewhat unsteadily should only be given one pint, or even no more than a half of lager shandy. People working in a difficult area can have 48 or 49 pints.*

Q: The head of our school is insisting that LMS requires massive changes in everyone's titles and duties. He has put to the governors a proposal that he should be renamed Absolute Supreme and Unchallenged Chief Executive and Ruler of the Universe and be given a pay rise of several thousand pounds. At the same time he is proposing to devolve most of his duties to myself, his deputy. Now he has ordered me to rename my job. I cannot think of a suitable title. If I am no longer to be called deputy head, can you suggest a good name for me in the future?

A: *Sucker.*

Q: I am not entirely clear where to find out about teachers' conditions of service. The LMS supplements mentioned some-thing about a Burgundy book for teachers and various kinds of books covering other people who work in the school. Can you clarify this?

A: *It is all quite straightforward. Teachers' conditions of service are published in what is known as the Burgundy book, because Burgundy is what you will need a bottle of two of, if you are ever foolish enough to try to read it. The secretaries' version is published in the Tasteful Lilac, Scented With Just A Hint of Miss Dior book. The conditions of service for PE teachers can be found in the Faded Loughborough Purple book and those for CDT teachers in the book with the leather patches on the spine. The deputy heads' version is published in the Extremely Sensible Black Shoes book. Caretakers' conditions of service are available in the Dark Brown With a Few Oily Stains book, which usually can't be found but is thought to be down in the boiler-room or somewhere about the site.*

Q: I have lost the very useful checklist from the LMS supplement on the maintenance of premises. Can you just remind me what it said?

A: *What is the state of the roof? (a) sound (b) in need of repair (c) no longer there. What are the walls like? (a) recently decorated (b) peeling (c) covered in rather primitive looking paintings of mammoths and sabre-toothed tigers. Who is responsible for the maintenance of your church school? (a) the vicar (b) the diocesan body (c) God knows. If you had £250 to spend on school repairs at the end of the financial year what would you do? (a) mend holes in the drive (b) buy a snooker table for the staffroom (c) put it all on a horse and gold plate the school if it came up.*

Q: Our local MP recently addressed a conference of school governors and told us that LMS will give us a lot more freedom. Can you spell out what this will actually be?

A: *Certainly. You will have freedom to go bankrupt if you overspend. You are free to devote all your spare time to raising extra money. You will be at liberty to spend six hours at governors' meetings trying to make ends meet. You also have complete freedom to have a nervous breakdown at any time of your own choosing.*

Q: I cannot remember the details now, but there was some mention in one of the supplements of a special group of individuals who may act as LEA trouble-shooters once LMS is in place. What do you call those people who will deal with schools' difficulties, bail the school out when there are cash-flow problems, rescue the governors if they are in danger of losing face, smooth things over with parents, and take the blame when things go wrong?

A: *Teachers.*

30 March 1990

It's a cock-a-hoop and bull story, Brian

SWINESVILLE BOTTOM OF LEAGUE: Today the *Swineshire Globe* publishes the first-ever Swineshire schools league tables in a special supplement sponsored by Doggifood plc, the dog food with the woof. Bottom of the Doggifood truancy league (see table 5 on page 2 of your *Swinesville Globe* league tables supplement) is Swinesville county primary school with a 100 per cent truancy record.

Chairman of governors, garage owner Ned Nock (55) declared himself to be 'sick as a parrot'. 'I'm gutted Brian,' he told our reporter. 'The name's Damian,' our reporter replied. 'We was robbed Brian,' continued Mr Nock, clearly distraught at the devastating news. 'The head put everyone down as absent on Good Friday by mistake, otherwise we would have kept a clean sheet.'

Today thousands of parents are eagerly combing the columns of the *Globe*'s special supplement to find out how their nearest and dearest have got on in the various Doggifood leagues.

The key to the columns in the league tables supplement is as follows:

Col 1: A-level scores.
Col 2: Percentage of pupils with five or more GCSE subjects at grade A to C.
Col 3: Deputy head's shoe size.
Col 4: Chairman of governors' IQ (to the nearest millimetre).
Col 5: Number of pet hamsters per class.
Col 6: Percentage of children whose parents vote Conservative.
Col 7: Number of dogs preferring Doggifood.

Top of the Doggifood A-level table is Upper Swineshire infants' school with an average points score of 96, equivalent to eight grade As and two grade Bs per pupil.

'We let the reception class children fill the forms in themselves, as it fitted in nicely with our personal and social education programme,' said headteacher Glenda Snooks (44), 'They really enjoyed themselves and they're tickled pink to be top of the A-level league.'

Happiest parent of the day was Mrs Mavis Fothergill (37) whose daughter put herself down for 15 grade As. 'This was a tremendous achievement by our Amanda,' said her mother proudly, 'especially as she's only on Ladybird book 2b.'

Winner of the deputy head shoe size league was Mr James Pettigrew (49), deputy head of the Lower Swineshire grant-maintained academy, with a whopping size 17. 'This shows that opting out pays off,' said Mr Pettigrew triumphantly. He denied allegations that he had deliberately let the cricket pitch roller run over his foot in a desperate bid to ensure Lower Swineshire came top of something.

There was only one winner when it came to the chairman of governors' lowest IQ scale, and that was Mr Alf Hardcastle (51) of Upper Swineshire junior school. 'I must be in a class of my own,' he said. 'We're all thick in my family, but I'm the daftest. First of all I think these league tables actually mean something, second I read all the papers for every single governors' meeting, and third I think John Patten is a really good bloke.'

A Department for Education spokesman described the league tables as a triumph for the Government's information revolution. 'This is a triumph for the Government's information revolution,' said Mr Henry Farnes-Barnes (59), reading from a prepared statement.

Asked why Swinesville girls' secondary modern school had come top of the GCSE league table, when it had in fact been closed down in 1967, Mr Farnes-Barnes said that it was the view of ministers that good schools never die.

Politicians were cock-a-hoop at the success of the league tables. John Patten (late forties, still maturing) told reporters: 'We define truancy as "unauthorised absence", and I am very keen on it. That is why I have been absent from most of the teacher union conferences.' He went on to talk about further work he hopes to see develop from the league tables. 'This exercise has been well worth the £10 billion we have spent on it.'

'For example, I have noticed that in schools where 100 per cent of pupils play truant every day, the exam pass rate is zero. It makes me wonder if there is any connection between the two things.'

Doggifood plc is also delighted with the success of its sponsorship. When asked how the company felt about the sponsorship of league tables generally, what was the official company response to criticisms of the blatant advertising of commercial products, and whether this trivialized what was meant to be a serious educational context, company spokesman Bowser (8) replied, 'Woof woof'.

□ Next November: The *Swineshire Globe* will bring you the 1994 league tables. Look out for tremendous improvements in the truancy figures as headteachers learn to play the smart game in their returns. See the breathtaking cheek as ministers claim their policies have been successful.

Watch this space.

3 December 1993

HOW WOULD YOU FIND OUT ABOUT EDUCATION POLICY WITHOUT THE TES?

Every week The Times Educational Supplement examines and debates the issues that matter to everyone with an interest in education.

Available every Friday at your newsagent or, if you would like to subscribe please send a cheque or credit card details to TES Subscriptions, PO Box 14, Harold Hill, Romford RM3 8EQ, or call our credit card hotline on 01708 378379.

Annual rates (52 issues):

UK £65, Europe and Eire £99,
USA and Canada (Air Freight) US$137,
Rest of the World (airmail) £150.

YOU CAN'T AFFORD TO IGNORE IT